"José Orduña's book violates—in a most exciting way—a number of literary borders: the political essay is enclosed within a novel; tough political observation is enlivened suddenly by a rush of metaphor or lush detail from the poet's eye; finally, humor and pathos meet on the page 'without papers.' Here is an exuberant, outlaw literary style that is the mix of several and that exactly matches the many ironies of being—and not quite ever being—a North American."

—RICHARD RODRIGUEZ,
AUTHOR OF *Brown: The Last Days of America*

"José Orduña's wonderfully wry, insightful, and beautiful debut is as deft as they come in nonfiction. *The Weight of Shadows* teeters on that dangerous nexus of race, class, and identity in American culture, charging through its subject matter with exhilarating confidence in order to bring us a mix of reportage, history, and autobiography that ultimately coalesces into a meditation on the physical, psychic, and aesthetic boundaries that taunt, challenge, and sometimes even inspire us all."

—JOHN D'AGATA,
AUTHOR OF *Halls of Fame: Essays*

"A beautifully written, insightful memoir that examines questions of citizenship and immigration with compassion, integrity, and fearlessness. *The Weight of Shadows* is an outstanding debut that instantly places Orduña among the ranks of literature's best new talent."

—JERALD WALKER,
AUTHOR OF *Street Shadows: A Memoir of Race, Rebellion, and Redemption*

D0090110

"In this timely and remarkably crafted work, José Orduña skillfully weaves personal memoir with deeply researched facts to reveal the disquieting truths no citizen of conscience can afford to ignore. A powerful meditation on the fraught road to naturalization, *The Weight of Shadows* awakens us to the privileges and burdens of Americanness and the troubling and often-dehumanizing abuses suffered by those in the 'shadows.'"

—SHULEM DEEN,
AUTHOR OF *All Who Go Do Not Return*

"José Orduña has written a provocative and insightful work that is destined to introduce a new form to the world of creative nonfiction. We have faith in his facts and Orduña essays us into a position of activism, documentation, and nuanced storytelling. *The Weight of Shadows* opens new pathways toward understanding the repercussions of our immigration policies, a counter-narrative to our media-skewed perceptions of a human rights issue that has no border. Orduña's hybrid approach to narrative employs the urgency of fiction, an investigative, reportorial eye, and a sublime, bilingual lyricism. This memoir will no doubt be required reading for years to come."

—WILLIE PERDOMO,
AUTHOR OF *The Essential Hits of Shorty Bon Bon*

THE WEIGHT OF SHADOWS

THE WEIGHT OF SHADOWS

A Memoir of Immigration & Displacement

José Orduña

BEACON PRESS

BOSTON

Beacon Press
Boston, Massachusetts
www.beacon.org

Beacon Press books
are published under the auspices of
the Unitarian Universalist Association of Congregations.

19 18 17 16   8 7 6 5 4 3 2 1

This book is printed on acid-free paper that meets the uncoated paper
ANSI/NISO specifications for permanence as revised in 1992.

Text design and composition by
Wilsted & Taylor Publishing Services

Some names and other identifying characteristics of people
mentioned in this work have been changed to protect their identities.

Library of Congress Cataloging-in-Publication Data

Names: Orduna, Jose.
Title: The weight of shadows : a memoir of immigration and
displacement / Jose Orduna.
Description: Boston : Beacon Press, [2016] | Includes bibliographical
references.
Identifiers: LCCN 2015031583| ISBN 978-0-8070-7401-5 (pbk. : alk.
paper) | ISBN 978-0-8070-7402-2 (ebook)
Subjects: LCSH: Mexican Americans—Biography. | Immigrants—
United States—Social conditions—21st century. | Hispanic
Americans—Civil rights. | Hispanic Americans—Social
conditions—21st century. | United States—Emigration and
immigration—Social aspects.

Classification: LCC E184.M5 O76 2016 | DDC 973/.046872—dc23
LC record available at http://lccn.loc.gov/2015031583

For Yolanda and Martín,

and for all those who refuse to live as shadows

CONTENTS

CHAPTER I

Imaginary Lines

Toward the tail end of the evening rush where Octavio and I work, three large men with sharp faces come through the back door. They move tactically, tracing a straight line through the dim dining room, their movements almost graceful as they glide past the museum-quality Morales and de Jesus paintings on the walls—fine art for the diners' consumption, to accompany tweezer-plated morsels prepared with color composition, textural variety, and playful temperature variances in mind. No one seems to notice these bulky men who never break stride. But I see that one man looks at people's hands, the second focuses on faces, and the third scans torsos. Smoothly turning their heads to survey the room, they look like feeding herons.

Returning to the host stand, I catch the gleam of an earpiece snaking down the third one's thick neck.

God, I think to myself, *to hear the voice on the other end.*

The gait of the man in the middle seems somewhat stunted, not so fluid as the others. Just before he turns a corner I think I notice a large geometric bulge under his jacket. I imagine it's some kind of submachine gun with switchable burst settings, designed for use in close quarters—like a dining room. I picture one of the customers being cut down by a short *fusillade*, penetrated by three rounds diagonally across the chest, or perhaps two individual rounds from two separate trigger squeezes.

The Swiss-made SIG Sauer P229 pistol chambered with .357 SIG rounds is an agency preference, its platform and round combination merging the accuracy of a nine-millimeter with the stopping power of the .357. *Stopping power*: the ability to transform a human into a corpse right where one stands, a hot metal projectile boring its way nine to fifteen inches into a human chest. This kind of power is given a rating based not only on the depth of the hole but by the size of the temporary stretch cavity it creates. The SIG's is forty-five cubic inches. Picture a hole in a chest the size of a Christmas ornament displacing connective tissue and organs, splintering bone. Stopping.

Catching a glimpse of Octavio clearing a table across the dining room, I smile and he returns a quick nod. I turn back toward the men, but they're gone. Octavio approaches the host stand and draws his face in just a few inches from mine.

"Qué pasa, cabrón?" he whispers.

"Obama." I motion toward the back table with my head.

The president has a standing reservation here. He gets the quiet table in the back corner near both rear exits. When he decides to come for dinner, a Secret Service agent sends the general manager a text message from a Type One device— Blackberry, probably—that's been certified by the NSA for transmitting classified government information. The text, perhaps just the word *Renegade*, will have run through several of the world's most complex algorithms before landing in the general manager's inbox. It might read *RRRR*, if Renaissance, Radiance, and Rosebud plan to join him for a family dinner.

Octavio walks to the wall that divides the two restaurants into discrete dining rooms, takes a look into the fine dining side, but doesn't go in. Busboys on that side wear ties and silk vests for the politicians, celebrities, and hedge fund managers. Seating is done by reservation only, filling at least three months in advance. You can order à la carte, but people usually opt for one of the three five-course tasting menus paired with whatever the sommelier recommends. The average diner drops around five hundred dollars for a meal.

Octavio dips back, clearing three tables before he's at the end of the regular dining room. Busboys from this side wear black guayaberas and never enter the other side. This rule doesn't even need to be stated because it is so concretely understood. For example, the dishwasher, El Conejo, is never seen outside his dish pit. He eats his shift meal standing above the industrial sink if he has time, or chugs the black coffee—two Splendas—I sneak him. When he's had too much caffeine he emerges, having frantically powered through a mountain of dishes only to hit a lull, which in turn makes him pop his head aggressively through the swinging doors of the pit, grab the first busboy who walks by, and growl, "Tráeme más platos, puto."

I go wherever I want because I speak English as if it were my mother tongue. Instead of a uniform, I wear Hermès ties with H's woven into their double-ply silk. When the maître d' for the fine-dining side is swamped, I'm allowed to give him a hand. I ask people, most white, if I may take their coats, handing them off immediately to a young Mexican woman who manages to remain out of sight until the very moment she's needed. I pull chairs out for women, wait until the men have taken their seats, then place open menus directly into everyone's hands.

When payroll makes an error on my check, I don't hesitate to take the elevator up to the corporate offices, knock on the head accountant's door, and kindly ask him for a moment of his time. Once, two pay cycles went by without me getting a paycheck, and the floor manager kept forgetting to do anything, telling me the problem would be sorted out by next payday. In his office, the accountant carefully looked at his screen and let out a forceful *hah*, as if trying to dislodge something in his airway. Seemed I'd been deleted from the digital clock-in system so that none of my hours had been logged.

"Well, how many hours did you work last month?" he asked, not especially perturbed.

There was no way for me to remember, I told him. I tried to picture the beginning of the month when I'd first gotten the job, thinking I'd be able to save enough money to move to Iowa for graduate school, put a deposit down on an apartment, and buy a $680 money order to send to the Department of Homeland Security with an N-400 form in order to initiate naturalization.

"Come on, come on," he said, flopping his big hands at me. "Just gimme a number."

I did some quick math. "A hundred forty?"

It was only slightly above what the real number must have been. Perfectly fair, though, I reasoned, considering the two pay cycles I'd had to wait. Without hesitation, the accountant took a fat wad of folded bills out of his slacks and counted out fourteen crisp hundreds, placing each one directly onto my open palm.

"You let me know if this happens again, kiddo."

Slowly placing the bills in my hand, the bookkeeper was perfectly genial, but I wondered if he didn't realize that this kind of error—missing hours, inaccuracies in pay rate, payroll system glitches—happens regularly, inevitably in the restaurant's favor. I wondered too if he failed to understand that the reason El Conejo in the dish pit and Octavio on the floor didn't come up to his office was because they'd been obliged, since their first jobs in the States, to grin and bear whatever, without saying a word. Men like Octavio and El Conejo might get their money eventually, after bills had moved into collection and accrued late fees; after they'd received calls from debt collectors making threats of repossession; after their gas was shut off, teaching them what a bitterly cold shower feels like at five in the morning, the same lesson their children would learn at six thirty when it was time to get ready for school.

In 2008 we would have been happy to see Obama walk quietly to his table—all that hope so neatly wrapped up in a black package. Now, however, three years later, when the three men reappear, posting themselves at three separate points in the dining room—two near the entrances and one sitting at the next table—it's different. We joke about him dropping dead after choking on his deconstructed taco.

There are two men at table fifty-six who I think might be on the job. They have the same thick bodies as the other three, and they have the same square hands, with fat thenar eminences that bulge after years of gripping things. They don't seem to be enjoying their luminous squares of perfectly cooked halibut, topped with cilantro foam, placed delicately on a disk of micro greens and edible flowers grown on the restaurant's rooftop garden. They don't seem to notice the hammered copper chargers underneath their plates. Neither one has touched the wine the sommelier poured.

My phone buzzes against my thigh, and as I take it out to check the blue voicemail symbol, I miss the presidential entrance.

He's sitting now, surrounded by a bunch of old white men. No Renaissance, no Radiance, no Rosebud. One of the men fingers the slightly angled silverware placed in front of him, nudging it back from the brink of chaos. Most of that cutlery was polished this morning by Octavio, an "illegal alien."

"Pinche Obama," he says, back at the host stand, shaking his head before he goes back to work.

Pinche Obama because Octavio had let himself believe that, being not white, the new president would necessarily be sympathetic to the plight of undocumented immigrants. Because he had let himself believe he and the US-born fiancée he's been engaged to for four years now would finally be able to get married.

At the very least we all thought something referred to as "the three ten bar"—introduced as a section of the Illegal Immigration Reform and Immigrant Responsibility Act, signed by Bill Clinton in 1996—would disappear. It didn't.

Purely a punitive tool, this legal category of "unlawful presence" was entirely new to immigration law. Individuals who accumulated six to twelve months of "unlawful presence" would be barred from the country for three years, while those here for more than a year would be barred for ten. So in order to adjust his immigration status when marrying his fiancée, Octavio would have to leave the country for up to ten years, which would mean losing the home he's paid a mortgage on for longer than a decade. The modest home his mother was having built in Mexico wouldn't be finished. Instead, she would have to share a one-room structure, made of cinderblock and corrugated tin, with Octavio's sister and his two nephews. As for his sweetheart in the United States, they might try to stay together while living in different countries, visit each other as often as possible, but the distance would become too great. They would begin to fight about any little thing, and then they would avoid talking for days at a time. For both of them, a day would come when they would quietly realize they no longer felt that pleasant attachment to the other—the intimacy of being together—and, soon after, their fifteen-year relationship would dissolve like sugar in warm milk.

We agree to meet at the bar next door after work. Octavio gets off an hour after I do, so I get started alone. El Conejo, having escaped his dish pit to join me, is leaning over the bar, rubbing his hands together, picking at dead skin, wincing. The right one is swollen and red, while the left one has thick, white scales that are raised at the edges. My dad has the same condition, several decades after being a dishwasher—hazards of one's hands spending twelve hours a day submerged in hot water and industrial-strength soap. I walk up behind him and swat him on the back.

"No mames, guey," he protests.

"First round's on me." He doesn't speak English but understands it comprehensively.

At the far end of the bar, one of the cooks leans his five-foot-three body across the pool table. He's about to sink the eight ball on our sous chef. There's a whole goat at stake for weekend birria. All the regulars are there, each slumped forward in a severe curve that renders even the tallest (six and a half feet when standing) diminutive on his stool. No one's fed the jukebox yet, so their cigarette-gnarled greetings rise above the sounds of clanking glass. I take my place at the end.

A Cuba libre seems the thing to have right now. It's Octavio's favorite, and once he shows up he won't let me drink anything else anyway. If I order bourbon he calls me Yankee, pronounced *Jahn-kie*. I try to tell him bourbon is from the South, but he just cuts me off: *Jahn-kie!* The bartender is on the other side of the bar, telling one of the regulars how his girlfriend broke up with him a week after he paid for her breast implants.

"Nice return on the investment, huh?"

My phone buzzes against my thigh for the second time. This means what it always means: my voicemail is full. To delete messages I press seven repeatedly. I don't even listen to them anymore. I know what they say. They'll all be from my mom. Hijo mío, she says by way of opening, not mi hijo, her very syntax re-creating the process of a mother embracing her son. Placing the word for *son* first, she then grabs urgently with what follows: *of mine*. The interplay of these words evokes the rush of possession, the physical pull of a

mother who hasn't seen her son in a long, long time. And
then, following this, always a question or statement about
eating: *Have you eaten yet? What did you eat today? I hope
you've eaten. Have you been eating good? I just deposited money
into your account so please eat something good.* Since moving
out of my parents' home it's become easier to forget that the
question of where meals were to come from wasn't always so
readily answered, easy to forget the evenings when, telling
me they'd already eaten at work, they would simply sit and
watch *me* eat.

I press seven and seven and seven again because I don't
even need to listen to know how, in a lowered voice, as if
someone were listening, she will end by saying, "Cuidado—I
love you," and know that one of the things she wants me to
be careful about is la migra.

Each long Monday afternoon, her day off, my mother sits
in her kitchen drinking black coffee, watching sparrows dart
by the feeder outside the window. She'll turn on Noticiero
Telemundo on the small television under the cereal cabinet
and watch Pedro Sevcec while she dunks Marías in her coffee, trying to get them to her mouth before they liquefy and
plop into her cup. It would be easy to attribute her news
preference to language, but as soon as the reports are done
she changes the channel to watch US sitcoms. Years ago it
was *Family Matters*, *Silver Spoons*, and *Dinosaurs*. I have no
idea what she's watching now.

If she chooses Telemundo over the English news broad-
casts, it's mainly to avoid the US media's endlessly broadcast
images of Latinos hopping fences, depicting us as a unified
deluge without end. On April 14, 2005, for instance, had
she been watching CNN, a network that purports to be "the
most trusted name in news," she would have caught an episode of *Lou Dobbs Tonight* titled "Border Insecurity; Criminal Illegal Aliens; Deadly Imports; Illegal Alien Amnesty."
Within the first minute she would have heard host Lou

Dobbs assert, "The invasion of illegal aliens is threatening the health of many Americans." A few moments later she would have heard CNN correspondent Casey Wian follow by asserting that "almost a half-million fugitive illegal aliens are loose in the United States today" before relaying ICE's plan to outfit low-risk "illegal aliens" with electronic monitoring devices.

"Hijos de su puta madre," my mother would have said, the María stopping halfway to her mouth, the portion she'd already dunked plopping back into her cup of coffee and spraying the front of her shirt.

Looking up at her screen she would have read "BROKEN BORDERS" and "DEADLY IMPORTS" across the bottom. She would have taken in the great Lou Dobbs sitting in front of his own large screen that also read "DEADLY IMPORTS" amid a foreboding blue smoke and a slanted caduceus—the staff carried by Hermes into the underworld, a staff entwined by two serpents, topped with open wings. This was a mistake, probably on the part of a production designer, and yet it's apt enough: the caduceus, often erroneously used in place of the rod of Asclepius, the symbol of medicine and healing, is in fact a symbol of commerce, theft, deception, and death.

Dobbs—US flag pinned to his lapel—introduced his segment by reminding us that he'd "already reported here on the tremendous burden that illegal aliens put upon our national health care system," before segueing into talk of the country's "rising fears that once-eradicated diseases are now returning to this country though our open borders." He warned portentously, "Those diseases are threatening the health of nearly every American, as well as illegal aliens themselves."

Dr. Madeline Cosman, introduced by CNN as a medical lawyer (although according to her later obituary she was a "medieval expert"), went on to say that there are "some enormous problems with horrendous diseases that are being brought into America by illegal aliens." The diseases mentioned by Cosman: tuberculosis, chagas disease, malaria, and leprosy.

CNN correspondent Christine Romans, sitting before the same screen—"DEADLY IMPORTS" and a slanted caduceus—explained to a baffled Dobbs how "suddenly, in the past three years, America has more than seven thousand cases of leprosy."

She nodded emphatically as she repeated: "Leprosy." After a solemn pause, she said with rehearsed lament: "In *this* country."

The camera cut to Dobbs sitting stoically appalled, brow furrowed, mouth ever so slightly agape. He took a moment to gather himself.

"Incredible."

As it turns out, the figures provided by Romans, based on Cosman's expertise, were flagrantly wrong. According to the US Department of Health and Human Services, there have been 7,124 new cases of leprosy reported in the United States, but this number corresponds to a thirty-year period, not a three-year period. In 2010, the number of new cases reported in the United States was only 294. And according to Health and Human Services, "Most [95 percent] of the human population is not susceptible to infection with M. leprae."

These are the moments, I imagine, when my mom grabs her phone to call me, because even though we're not "illegals," she feels that these reports refer to us too because in this cultural moment, *illegal*—used as a noun—and the phrases *illegal alien* or *illegal immigrant* don't conjure a white face of European descent but a brown face much like mine. And it is very hard to hide your face.

By the time Octavio walks into the bar, I'm two drinks in but ready to keep going. We order another round.

"You're late."

"Así trabaja el indio." That is how the Indian works. A colloquialism.

We clink glasses.

One Friday night after a particularly grueling workweek, we're hanging out at Octavio's place, and he tells me how he crossed the border, something he's referred to often but never told me about in detail. We start the evening with music and some black market Havana Club with plenty of ice. He grabs his jarana, a small guitar-shaped instrument with eight strings. The body is made of cedar; the strings are stretched guts. Nuzzling it, placing his fingers on the fretted neck, he strums it hard, almost violently. I remember meeting him in Mexico, when I was eleven. He was playing with a twelve-man band that included a man-sized harp, the first I'd ever seen up close, several percussion instruments I didn't even know existed, like an ass's jaw, and four or five different instruments that resembled a guitar.

Octavio takes a nip of his rum and messes with the tuning pegs, turning each one slightly back and forth. He strums a few chords while angling his ear down toward the instrument. Getting the sound he's looking for, he smiles, takes one more nip from his cup, and then launches into "La Guacamaya," a classic Son Jarocho that takes two people to call and respond and is usually accompanied by a harp or jarana. The song, one I learned as a child in Chicago, is from my birthplace.

He starts by plucking the strings in a delicate and complicated melody that rises and falls for a few bars before a forceful strum marks the beginning of the driving rhythm characteristic of Son Jarocho. The sound is transformed from something one would expect from an Ibero-influenced string instrument to a percussive African drive, and, abetted by the porcupine quill Octavio uses to pick, it arrives at the sound particular to Veracruz.

He starts, and we alternate verses, singing about an unfortunate macaw that has to fly away when all his dragon fruit is gone. Midway through, Octavio's fiancée pounds on the wall from her bedroom, so we shut up.

He asks me if I ever miss Veracruz. "Not exactly," I tell him. The truth is I don't remember living there, but it does maintain a vague and powerful grip on me. Octavio says he misses it. It's been more than fifteen years since he saw his mother, and although he doesn't overtly say it, it's clear that he's scared he won't ever get to see her again.

"Everyone has the right to leave any country, including his own," according to the Universal Declaration of Human Rights. But when Octavio left, he wasn't accepted anywhere. People are free to go but not arrive, making this declaration another example of the hollow rhetoric of human rights in international law. He was given a note card with a Tijuana address scribbled on it, two thousand miles from his home in Veracruz, and told to be there two days later.

"Pues le dije adiós a todos."

Putting down the jarana, Octavio pours us another drink. They're getting stronger, the ice cubes reduced to slivers floating in pale rum that tastes more and more like salted caramel.

A man opened the door, he recounted: "El tipo se veía de mala calaña."

He noticed the man's nostrils were raw, and he seemed strung out. He had scabs on his face and kept scratching a small area of his jeans, the denim there looking lighter and thinner than the rest of his pants. The man showed him to a small room with a stained mattress on the floor. They told him to stay in there and that they would get him when it was time. Every two days they brought him a liter of water and several containers of leftover carryout. Six days went by.

"Nos metieron como a seis en una cajuela."

Six adult men were packed into the trunk of a small vehicle, a Corolla or something, and then a stranger drove them for hours on dark highways toward an unknown destination. They had been told to carry as little as possible and told that if they were at any point spotted, they were on their own. At one point, one of the men in the trunk got a calf cramp, but there wasn't enough room for him to extend his leg, or even reach it, so another man kneaded it for him.

And then, sometime later, the car just stopped. Someone opened the trunk, and led them into total darkness. Each step for miles was taken in complete uncertainty, and each footfall landed with violent shifting. After several hours they came to an embankment with a steep gravel drop. In the distance, lights snaked down a highway and bled into the ditch on their side. They could hear the rushing sound of traffic beyond them but couldn't pick their heads up to see the cars. It sounded like a river to Octavio, or like the sound of wind moving through the dry cornstalks he used to listen to as a child.

They hid in a thicket. One of the men put a cigarette in his mouth and struck a lighter once before the *pollero* slapped it away. A few moments later, one of the other men noticed someone from the group was missing. They discussed having seen him at the last stop they had made, about half an hour back.

"El pollero quería seguir, pero lo mandamos a la chingada."

One man decided to go back, while the others waited in silence in the brush. When the man returned, he just shook his head. "Ya no," he said.

They ran across a twelve-lane highway, and when they reached the other side, a squadron of border patrol agents popped out from underneath a pile of garbage bags where they'd been hiding. Octavio and the other men were confronted with a wall of men in dark tactical gear and assault rifles.

A boot pressed down on the side of Octavio's head, crushing his ear. The men were placed in the dog cage mounted on the back of the border patrol vehicle and then were taken to a booking station. Octavio could hear the *pollero* vomiting in the next cell, while another man attempted to tell the officers that their friend's body was somewhere in the desert. One of the agents gave Octavio a Coca-Cola and smiled at him— told him in broken Spanish that things would turn out okay. Hours later they scanned his fingertips and had him sign some papers, most likely a voluntary departure form. He was loaded on a bus and driven for hours to a Mexican port of entry far from where he had attempted to cross. He was unloaded. An officer removed his cuffs and pointed toward the entrance of a building. It was not yet dawn, but the structures in the distance started to gain the vaguest of contours.

After my final night of work at the restaurant, after a meal of sliced duck breast in mole negro, and after several glasses of snuck tequila that retails at about fifty dollars a shot, I remembered only three things: dancing with two very tall, very attractive Russian women to a Cuban bolero, taking a deep and caustic drag of an American Spirit lit at the wrong end, and Octavio shaking my hand with a folded hundred-dollar bill in his: a hard-earned contribution toward my citizenship. "Qué esperas, cabrón?"

CHAPTER 2

Martín y Yoli

*Future generations of Americans will be thankful
for our efforts to humanely regain control of our
borders and thereby preserve the value of one
of the most sacred possessions of our people:
American citizenship.*

—Ronald Reagan

When Martín became my father, he was skinny. He isn't fat
now, but there's a photo of him from that time in which he's
bathing a black puppy in a washbasin, and in it he looks like
a lanky kid. Somehow, even though he was about to have a
child himself, he looks placid. His arms look relaxed, and he's
holding the wet puppy very gently. He looks present in that
moment, like his mind is occupied with nothing other than
kneading suds into a puppy's back with his thumbs.

The person taking the photo, maybe Martín's mother
Estela, may have captured a moment of genuine calm, or it
may just seem that way to me because I'd like to imagine
they weren't devastated by the news that they'd soon be parents; I know how I would have felt about it at his age, twenty.
Or maybe the photo was taken just before anyone knew.

The puppies—two white, two black—were only a few
weeks old, and they lived in a cardboard box lined with

blankets. The box was in an entryway that led to the courtyard of the family home in Fortín. I remember seeing the photo for the first time when I was eight and being really drawn to three large metal tanks nestled between pots of young anthuriums. They looked like helium tanks for balloons, and my mom explained that they were filled with gas for the house, that in Fortín there was a truck that rode around town delivering them door to door, with a guy on the back shouting "Gas!" My mom said it was the same gas that came through the pipes in our place in Chicago and heated the oven, and I wondered whether those pipes were connected to tanks of gas somewhere in the basement of our apartment building. My mom said the gas came from the utility company, that there was a whole world of pipes and wires underneath the city, and that she didn't really know exactly how it all worked, but it didn't work like it worked in Mexico.

They always referred to Mexico. How this was different in Mexico or how that was oddly similar in Mexico, and I got some idea but never really a complete picture of what it meant. I had no recollection of it at all, just the sense that being from there affected almost every aspect of how we lived in Chicago. It had to do with why we didn't answer the phone sometimes and why my dad wouldn't say anything when they shorted him some hours at work, even though we really needed that money. It had to do with why they worked him thirty days in a row or more, why some people whose names I knew called themselves something different when they went to work, and why my grandparents, like most of my extended family, were complete strangers to me.

Yoli had been majoring in agronomy, with one semester left, when she found out she was pregnant and had to quit school. Her father kicked her out, and she went to live with Martín's family. Before this she'd been interested in soil science, in how land can become depleted and lose its ability to produce food. She knew how to graft plants. There was a tree near her home that had been pink, and she added a branch of white blossoms that took. She never told anyone about it so it could be her secret to look at every time she passed. She was also athletic and got along better with her two brothers than with her three sisters. She'd grown to love basketball because her brother loved basketball, and her mother rarely let her out of the house except to play with him and to run errands. She had a broad back and muscular shoulders because in high school she'd been a swimmer, and she could do six wide-grip pull-ups in a row.

Yolanda's mother, María, beat Yoli but none of her siblings. I didn't know about this until well into my teens. María died young, of lung cancer, and Yoli had been the one to empty her bedpan, and she was the one who was there in her mother's last moments of agony. Somehow I'd always known things had not been good for her. I think it was that we never really talked about my grandparents. When we did it was brief, and we would always reach a point where my mother would become agitated and clam up. We talked about María and my grandfather, Pablo, so infrequently that sometimes, embarrassed, I'd have to be reminded what their names were. There weren't any pictures of them in our home.

By all accounts, Martín had a drinking problem. He wasn't the type of guy who woke up shaking, reaching for a drink, but when he drank it sometimes went on for days. We're similar in this way, and people say he was similar to his father in the same way. He had been in accounting, but by his own admission he wasn't any good at school, probably because he liked drinking so much. His father had only been around for a brief period at the beginning of Martín's life. He only saw him one time after that. His mother was Estela, and he called his uncle Roméo his father. He referred to him most frequently as Pa. Estela owned a restaurant, VicMar, which was a combination of her sons' names, Victor and Martín. They started working there when they were seven and five, and before they moved into their house in Fortín, they lived in a vecindad, a kind of housing arrangement for poor families where private rooms surround a shared courtyard, kitchen, and bath. Martín was friends with Pablo, the brother with whom Yoli played basketball, and that's how they met. But really they'd always sort of known each other, and then one day things were just different. Neither of them can say what it was really, but they started hanging out alone, without telling anyone. They listened to Silvio Rodriguez on Martín's record player, and Yoli enjoyed being away from her family.

Martín was Yoli's first real boyfriend.

Her nipples itched. Martín noticed that she'd been scratching them a lot lately. They were on a day trip with Victor and his girlfriend, Marta, on the coast. They all noticed that Yoli was fidgeting with her flannel shirt but thought, at first, that it was the wool. It wasn't the wool. After she changed into a cotton T-shirt but kept fidgeting, Martín asked Yoli if she had been regular.

Regular?

They said when they found out, it was clear what they needed to do.

Martín's aunt, Hilda, had moved to Chicago a few years before. A friend of hers from Fortín lived in Chicago and worked as a housekeeper for a wealthy family. When one of their other housekeepers quit, they asked the friend if she knew anyone who wanted to fill the spot. "Someone like you," they'd said, meaning a Mexican, rather than a black person, not understanding that there are black Mexicans, so they sponsored Hilda's arrival and got her a green card just like that.

We would always have a complicated relationship with Chicago, but it's where I first remember coming into consciousness. Martín had gone to the United States before us, to get a job and save some money. He got here in the winter, and the coat he imagined would be enough wasn't. The first steps he took outside of the airport were into negative-ten-degree cold. Before that, the coldest he'd ever experienced was around forty degrees, when he climbed with Yoli's brothers to the peak of Citlaltépetl, where he saw snow for the first time. He didn't know that cold could hurt inside, and he could feel on that first Chicago night that cold could very easily stop him from living. It was nighttime, and before his aunt Hilda arrived to pick him up, he felt alone in a strangely familiar way. It was a feeling he associated with Manuel, his biological father. He didn't know when he would see his wife and baby again. When he thought about this something turned between his ribs and his heart. A man outside the airport asked him something in English, he just shook his head, *No.*

Martín arrived in the United States on the cusp of shifting sentiment, a flux that was consistent with history. In 1921, the US Congress passed the Emergency Quota Act, which restricted the flow of southern and eastern European immigrants, and in 1924 the Immigration Act restricted the flow of eastern and southern Asians. Mexicans, however, were excluded from these and weren't really considered immigrants but laborers. The agriculture lobby had been successful in insuring that Mexicans were allowed to come and go with the seasons because they were cheap and pliant, so many of them did. Others settled. When the Great Depression hit, between four hundred thousand and two million Mexicans and Mexican Americans, many of whom were US citizens, "left" the United States. This period, known as the Mexican Repatriation, isn't widely known by the general public. Repatriation usually referred to the official process by which the now defunct Immigration and Naturalization Service (INS) returned someone to his or her country of origin or citizenship, but a relatively low number of the people expelled during this period were expelled through INS-directed removal. The administrative process of deportation was not as fully developed and institutionalized as it is today. Instead, the lives of many Mexicans and Mexican Americans were made untenable when the federal government provided support for, and turned a blind eye to, draconian state and local government initiatives like conducting arbitrary raids on Latino communities, wrongfully removing US citizens, and securing "transportation arrangements with railroads, automobiles, ships, and airlines to effectuate wholesale removal of persons out of the United States to Mexico." Mexican and Mexican American communities were "forced to abandon, or were defrauded of, personal and real property, which often was sold by local authorities as 'payment' for the transportation" to Mexico.

Mexicans and other people perceived as foreigners were blamed for taking jobs from white people in the United States during the period after World War I. This accelerated during the Great Depression even though many of the areas where the blame occurred had been Mexican territory less than a century before, and Mexican labor had been a boon to the economy there. State and local law enforcement officials also turned a blind eye to systemic racist violence aimed at purging foreigners. Most Mexicans' departures were officially categorized as voluntary, but in reality they left under threat of violence. Methods of coercion existed on a spectrum ranging from formal (increased official deportation by the INS during the 1930s) to informal (Mexican laborers dragged from fields by angry mobs, tortured, and killed). V. Wayne Kenaston Jr., a San Diegan whose parents were members of their local chapter of the Ku Klux Klan during this period, remembered that "years ago east of 55th Street and El Cajon Boulevard, past College Avenue, there were lemon orchards." The bodies of murdered Mexicans would occasionally be discovered among the trees, "sometimes disfigured by torture."

The context in which the Mexican Repatriation happened was already one steeped in racist terror. As historians William D. Carrigan and Clive Webb point out in their research on lynching,

> Statistics alone can never explain lynching in the United States. More than other Americans, blacks and Mexicans lived with the threat of lynching throughout the second half of the nineteenth and the first half of the twentieth century. The story of Mexican lynching is not a footnote in history but rather a critical chapter in the history of Anglo western expansion and conquest.

In their research, Carrigan and Webb note that numbers for Mexican victims of lynching are extremely difficult to collect because most were never recorded, and the victims that were recorded were often racially misclassified. The definition of lynching itself has shifted over time, and in their count Carrigan and Webb call lynching "a retributive act of murder for which those responsible claim to be serving the interests of justice, tradition, or community good." According to Carrigan and Webb, the rate of black Americans lynched from 1880 to 1930 was 37.1 per 100,000. The rate of Mexican lynching during the same period was 27.4 per 100,000.

Mexico's history has always been inextricably linked to that of the United States. Yoli says that growing up she often heard her father repeat a saying: "¡Pobre México! Tan lejos de Dios y tan cerca de los Estados Unidos." The quote is popularly attributed to Porfirio Díaz, which is dubious but possible since Díaz would have been eighteen years old in 1848 at the conclusion of the US invasion of Mexico, which ended with the Treaty of Guadalupe Hidalgo, in which the United States took about half of Mexico's landmass, including all of California. With the signing of the treaty, Mexicans living on the wrong side of the newly established boundary lost property rights along with any semblance of civic power; they were segregated, and their culture deemed worthless and deviant.

The saying coming from Díaz makes less sense if you consider that the United States supported his dictatorship because it was in their economic and political interest to do so. Some historians argue that "by the dawn of the twentieth century the United States controlled the Mexican economy." Because of mounting popular pressure, Díaz announced that Mexico was ready for democracy and agreed to hold free elections in 1909, during which he would run for his eighth term. William Howard Taft, the twenty-seventh president of the United States, met with Díaz at the El Paso–Juarez border in a historic show of solidarity for the "identical aims and ideals" of both nations. This wasn't surprising because "according to US Consular General Andrew D. Barlow, 1,117 US-based companies and individuals had invested $500 million in Mexico," and dictatorial rule had been good for this kind of American involvement. To Taft and US investors, the plethora of horrors created by the Porfiriato—like widespread debt slavery and Yaqui people being forced into labor camps—mattered little.

Popular resistance to Díaz grew, and Francisco I. Madero, an opposition candidate, ran in the election. Madero had gained widespread support, so much so that when the government announced the official election result, a landslide victory for Díaz, it was widely believed to have been fraudulent, and the Mexican Revolution broke out in 1910. The people of Mexico went to war with the ruling class, of which Díaz was a key representative.

During Madero's triumphant march to take the presidency there was an earthquake that produced cracks in the national palace—an omen of things to come. Madero had been a figure of opposition during the revolution, but soon after becoming the first new president in over thirty years it became clear to his former allies and to the Mexican people that he had been a revolutionary in name only. He kept many of the Díaz-created power structures in place and refused to institute policy that would challenge the hegemony of the wealthy landowning class, to which he and his family belonged. Díaz had been exiled to Paris soon after the revolution broke out, and the United States continued to support the regime most favorable to its economic interests. Henry Lane Wilson, the US ambassador to Mexico, became concerned that Madero would overturn the policies instituted by Díaz that had created foreign dominance of oil, mining, and railroads in Mexico. Shortly after the transition of power, there was a coup orchestrated in part by Wilson and led by Mexican general Victoriano Huerta. When it was over, Madero was dead, and Huerta declared himself president.

By 1935 most of the oil-producing companies in Mexico were foreign-owned. Sixty percent of oil production came from the Mexican Eagle Company, which was a subsidiary of the Royal Dutch Shell Company, and another 30 percent came from Jersey Standard and Standard Oil Company of California (now Chevron). It wasn't until 1938 that Lázaro Cárdenas expropriated the assets of nearly every foreign oil company operating in Mexico, to which the United States, Great Britain, and the Netherlands reacted by boycotting Mexican exports. But the US government quickly backed off when war clouds rolled in across the Atlantic, casting ambiguous shadows on the Americas.

In all the photographs of my first birthday, Martín is conspicuously missing. After Yoli had gotten kicked out of her house for becoming pregnant, she moved in with Martín's family while he worked in fields more than two thousand miles away. I spent the first months of my life in a house full of old people—my grandmother and her three brothers—

who were in an almost constant state of elation at their first grandchild being available to them after work each day.

On several occasions I've tried to gently ask Yoli how she felt then, asking if she felt lonely when I really meant abandoned. She's always said it wasn't a lonely time, because she lived with four people who considered themselves grandparents, and my actual grandmother was so doting and intuitive, but I'm not sure I believe her. Her mother had already passed away, and she says by that time she'd learned not to care about her father, but I don't know if I think that's possible. It must have injured her or, if she'd gotten so good at suppressing things, it must have dragged behind her like a plow.

"En esos días eras como la chingada," says Yoli, looking at a washed-out photo of her holding me above my huge white birthday cake.

She says right around then I'd started pointing with my index, and right before pointing I'd stare at the tip of my finger and pucker my lips, so she knew when it was coming. She'd started asking me how old I was right when she could tell I was going to point anyway, just for laughs. In the photo my index is up, and in the background all my aunts and uncles are laughing and cheering. She tells me this as we're sitting on her couch in my parents' rented apartment in Bucktown. She hands me the photo, which is slightly warped. I'm helping her put the rest of our old pictures into albums because right before they moved here there was a flood in their old house. The box of photos was on top of a small toolbox. If the water had been an inch higher we would have lost more than a decade of memories. Yoli had started putting them into albums, but the process was slowed because humidity had seeped into the box, and many of the pictures fused together. She'd laid the fused ones out on the living room floor, allowing them to dry in the sun before she started gently peeling them apart.

The moisture made many of the figures in the pictures

unrecognizable. Some were no more than sheets of blossoming color that looked more like exploding nebulae than the artifacts of a human life. And in a way they were similar: they represented the destruction of many realities. Without the photos, the particularities of our collective events would fade and continue to fade until the entirety of the events themselves would be lost to oblivion. For the time being, Yoli is able to make out what had been in the ruined photos: the entrance to the gazebo in the town square where we lived, my uncle Victor dressed in his white medical school uniform just a few weeks before the car accident that mangled his left hand, a small patch of grass where I took my first steps.

She hands me a stack of photos and explains that I should group them on the living room floor in some kind of order—whatever seems related—as best I can. The task is surreal because the home where they'd been living for the last five years was repossessed, and they scrambled to find an apartment with their bad credit. This, the only place they were able to get, was the apartment Martín's aunt Hilda had first lived in when she moved to the United States more than thirty years earlier. When Yoli and I arrived, we'd moved in next door. One of the first photographs in the stack is of Yoli stuffing me into a bright blue snowsuit during my first Chicago winter. My arms stick straight out, and we're standing in the very spot where we're now sitting over two decades later. My mom is a lot thinner in the photo, but she still has her full head of black hair that looks like wire, and there still isn't a single white one. I wonder whether she thinks it was all worth it. It seems, in this moment, like some circle has closed, like my mom and dad are exactly where they started, and for a moment I want to acknowledge this. I think about asking if she would do it again knowing how things turn out, but I decide it's a cruel and stupid question.

They knew it would be hard, but people really don't understand what that means until it becomes their life, and even then there's no understanding. It just becomes the condition in which you live. Staying would have meant growing up in the conditions post NAFTA and after Calderón and Clinton's declaration of war on drugs. In a letter Martín wrote on the occasion of my first birthday, knowing Yoli would be the one to read it, he says he hadn't expected to feel so bad. "The solitude feels like it's in my body. I don't feel physically well. Nothing is like *over there*." Nothing. He still hasn't found a place that sells the small avocados with the skin you can eat, and he can't tell when people are insulting him, but it feels as though they are all the time. "A million differences cascade into each other," he writes, "until you find yourself in a strange place and even *you* have become difficult to recognize."

In high school, when I started smoking weed and going to parties instead of studying, they would invoke the sacrifice they'd made in coming here. "How could you?" they asked. But I couldn't understand what they meant. I didn't want to be able to feel the weight of that kind of sacrifice, so I avoided thinking about anything that might lead me toward feeling this. And sometimes like a pinprick I would become acutely aware of that possibility, and instinctively I would do anything to get rid of that feeling as quickly and completely as possible.

Their plan had always been to send me to school. That was it. A good school. And somehow they made it happen. Along with photos, they keep documents and small trinkets in that same cardboard box. Yoli hands me a few pieces of crisp white paper folded in thirds:

BILL TO: Mr. M. Orduna and Mrs. Y. Gonzalez
BILL FOR: Orduna, Jose
TOTAL CHARGES: 11799.50.

She says it's like the pictures some people take at the top of mountains, and while I understand her pride, part of me cringes in thinking about how this aspect of our lives is used to advance the idea of the merit-based structure of the so-called American dream.

"Cómo va la aplicación?" asks Yoli.

"Bien."

After two weeks of logging onto the US Citizenship and Immigration Services website, I'd finally clicked on the link to download the PDF version of the N-400. After that it was another two weeks before I opened the file, only to immediately close it. I'd dragged it to my desktop, but just looking at the icon produced a fluttering in my ribs, so I'd kept a window open over it. I had to get a little drunk in order to finally start putting my information on the lines. Growing up I watched Yoli execute a similar maneuver with piles of envelopes that came in the mail. Martín was a dishwasher, and Yoli was a nanny to two boys. We didn't live in the worst neighborhood, but we were not unfamiliar with things like shootings. One night a young man was shot in the throat while he was sitting in front of our building, and we heard him screaming as he bled out on the sidewalk. Martín and Yoli decided they would send me to the local parochial school and would somehow make that work, so when the bills trickled in throughout the month, Yoli was in charge of trying to manage an impossible situation.

Sometimes she was able to manage, but other times it was too much, so she would stuff the envelopes in a drawer and avoid looking inside until she went to stuff another one in and couldn't because the drawer was full. Then she would open all the envelopes, grab the phone, and in a frantic purge pay as many of them as she could. The ones she was able to pay she tossed aside, and the others were shuffled around the table and put through a mysterious but exacting system she seemed to have worked out over the years. She'd call the various utility companies, creditors, or the landlord to try to negotiate more time. Sometimes she had to decide what necessity we would go without.

I remember always being aware of our money situation— we didn't have any—but not really having a clear sense of how our lives were different than other people's. It didn't really become clear until I reached high school. Yoli recently told me when she used to take me to the toy store, even when I was really young, it would break her heart to see me tear down the aisles until I saw something I liked. I'd slow down and become quiet. When she'd get to where I was, I'd be standing in front of the toy I wanted. I would take her by the hand and ask: "Hay dinero?"

The day of the entrance exam at Saint Ignatius, I walked under an archway covered in ivy. To the right, on a perfectly kept patch of grass, lay a twenty-foot slab of ornately carved stone. Later, after being accepted, I learned it was the only remaining piece of cornice from Louis Sullivan's old Chicago Stock Exchange, which had been demolished in 1965. I sat in the last row of my exam room, behind a tall girl named Chloé, and periodically I'd peak behind me out a window that looked down onto a brick courtyard with tendrils of ivy snaking up the exterior walls and a few benches nestled between flowered bushes. It was a meditation garden. I'd never met a Chloé, and I'd never imagined going to a high school with a meditation garden that looked like something from a Victorian novel.

Throughout my high school search, Martín and Yoli had been at an almost complete loss. They didn't know anything about the process or even that it *was* a process, and both were working fifty- or sixty-hour weeks. A day before the entrance exam, my middle school principal called me into her office and handed me a note card with an address on it. She said it was for Saint Ignatius and that I should go there and take the test. She asked if I'd be able to get a ride. I think she may have given me a calculator to use. When Martín pulled up in front of the sprawling grounds the following morning, he blurted out "holy shit," wished me luck, and gave me a kiss on the forehead.

I immediately felt the space to be severe. The original buildings were done in the Second Empire style, so the school resembles a palace. The main edifice is listed in the National Register of Historic Places. It's symmetrical, with a central tower and a mansard roof, vaguely French and slightly Baroque. Entering from Roosevelt Road one passes a ten-foot statue of Father Arnold Damen SJ, a Belgian Jesuit who founded Saint Ignatius after having been in the Dakotas converting Native peoples. He was alleged to have personally "saved" twelve thousand souls. Outside the lunchroom there's a fifteen-foot cast bronze herald blowing his horn, a statue that used to be on the Chicago Herald Building built by Burnham and Root. The main hallway is lined with framed photographs of each graduating class. Every small face is of a dead white man until a quarter of the way down the hall when white women are admitted. Farther down, the faces of people of color begin to emerge.

I don't think I was fully conscious of it at the time, or maybe I did my best to ignore it, but moving into those spaces early in the morning, and staying in them for most of the waking day, wasn't without its effects. I'd never felt as poor or as brown as I did against that "stark white background." At the time, we were living in a $700-a-month apartment. I slept on a mattress on the floor of a room slightly bigger than a closet. The floor in the kitchen was so warped that when one of us dropped a round fruit or vegetable it would roll in several directions before settling in a divot or ending up in a corner. There was a stretch when we had to take showers at the local park because we didn't have gas to heat water.

That period was of discomfortingly high contrast. I made friends with a Ukrainian transfer student named Alexy, who lived in a Gold Coast high-rise that overlooked the Chicago River and Navy Pier. I remember the first time we rode up the elevator to his place. The attendant who opened the door for us, two fifteen-year-old boys, called us "sirs." He was a middle-aged Mexican man whose accent was as thick as Martín's. It was a short ride, but inside the elevator time crept. Beads of sweat gathered on my skin, and I felt as though I was being observed, not by my friend, who was rather oblivious, but by the building itself and by the employees, who seemed to look at me a moment longer than at Al. It was a similar feeling I had walking through the halls of Ignatius, except there it seemed more diffuse. At school I felt the general obliviousness that comes with being a teenager, and I'd made friends with Simón and Sebastián, the two Mexican custodians at Ignatius. Saying hello and joking with them in the halls made me feel slightly less alienated because they felt less foreign to me than some of my affluent Mexican classmates.

That evening Al and I took rips from his plastic bong while sitting cross-legged on his balcony overlooking the river. In his building's indoor pool we bobbed up and down in lukewarm water watching the sun disappear behind a geometry of glass and metal. The skyline went red for a few minutes, and the marijuana helped shut down the part of my mind that was conscious of myself in this space. That kind of awareness—of my circumstances, of my parents—sloughed off, and I transitioned into a purely sensual few hours: my body feeling itself floating and my mind capable only of feeling the movements of water. My mind was temporarily evacuated of a caustic memory, desire, and awareness of being.

Later that evening, Al's dad came home from work with a paper bag full of "goodies" as he called them and insisted that I stay for dinner. He reached into the brown bag and placed several items on the kitchen counter. A block of tan butcher paper was unwrapped, and he sliced into a white slab of cured fatback called salo. A small golden jar with Russian characters and the image of a large sturgeon on the label was placed in the middle of an iridescent dish. Al retrieved a small mother-of-pearl spoon from a cupboard and slid it into the shiny black spheres in the open jar. His father poured us shots of vodka and told us to drink and eat, while he boiled dumplings.

"Mom, I don't know what's going to happen with us in the next few days, if I can fix my papers well there's hope in being here, but if I don't fix anything, I don't know what I'm going to do." This is in a Mother's Day letter that Martín wrote to Estela on May 5, 1988. He was twenty-five years old. "Anyway," he continues, "I think we'll be seeing each other really soon, whatever happens, I'll call to let you know." Throughout the letter he tells his mom things had become very hard and apologizes for giving her nothing but bad news. "Telling you really helps."

Yoli sees me reading the letter, and without looking very closely she knows which one it is. She's still grouping pictures on the floor and hands me one of Estela taken at a bit of a distance as she walks down a hill with her back to the camera. I don't immediately think anything of it and put it down on the couch next to which I'm sitting. Yoli says that Orduña, as she calls him, never sent the letter.

"Why not?" I ask.

She shrugs.

I pick up the photo again and when I do, it strikes me that when I'd seen it moments earlier I'd immediately and casually known who it was. Looking at it again, I wonder how since the picture is so small, a four-by-five, and Estela is even smaller in it, with her back to the camera. The hill isn't the one in front of her house—the one that leads to the park—it's just an asphalt street with white gates and foliage on both sides, and there's nothing recognizable about the location, nothing indicating that it was taken in Fortín. I look closely at the woman in the picture, and I can't even tell how old she may be. She's wearing a long navy skirt and a cardigan, so the only part of her body that's really visible is the skin on the back of her lower calves. The more I look at it, the more I begin to doubt it's her.

"Who is this?" I ask Yoli.

"Ay, come on," she says.

I ask her again why he never sent the letter, and she says things were very difficult then, and that he probably intended to but just forgot. It was written on letterhead from the Bismarck Hotel, where he worked as a dishwasher. Yoli says they had him working like "dos paisas," two countrymen, two Mexicans, and that still he had holes in his shoes. She says that's when he started to get "that thing," and she scratches and picks at the palm of her right hand, mimicking something I've seen him do so many times I don't notice it anymore. His right hand is white and has terrible scales that he picks until his palm has hollowed craters that look like the strata in a quarry. He's been to several doctors who ran tests and told him different things. When I was twelve he went to one who gave him pills that might fix his hand but also damage his liver, so he didn't take them. Whatever it is, Yoli says it started then, when his hands would be submerged in hot water and industrial cleaners for twelve or thirteen hours a day. She said when he got home they'd be white and swollen, like the skin under a bandage, damp for too long, except it was his whole hand up to the wrist. Then they would dry and turn bright red and scale, and she says she could tell they really hurt him at first but that after a while the pain no longer fazed him.

Yoli starts to get up from sitting cross-legged on the floor. She manages to get to one knee, and then she pauses for a moment. She's not even fifty, and she's in good health, but about a decade ago I'd seen her jump into a full-court pickup game of basketball with teenagers and guys from the neighborhood half her age. Brief pauses in movement like the one she just took remind me that my parents are aging, and they haven't been able to amass anything secure or permanent. They're back in this apartment, and the most valuable thing they own is their car, and it's not even that valuable. This specific thought, the realization they have nothing—a thought I have often, even more so as *I* become older—produces a very particular feeling. It's like a long crochet needle is being inserted under my ribs until it reaches my lung and then whomever is holding the needle begins to torque, using my bottom rib for leverage. And even though I know they experience much more than just pain, the way they still exist in the world pains me.

She walks back into the living room holding two cups of black coffee and a concha with the white, not the yellow, paste on top. She motions to the window where she's placed an array of small glass bottles I'd collected as a young boy. She always reminds me that for some reason I was obsessed with small glass bottles, and if we saw one somewhere it was impossible to get me out of the store without buying it. I remember the feeling of being drawn to them, and when I see them on the sill, I feel the remnant of that original sensation. It was something about the smoothness of the glass in my hand, but also about the novelty of their smallness. She's filled them all with water and there are cuttings from some of her plants growing and snaking up the window frame toward the sun.

"What was Pop talking about?" I ask, referring to the trouble Martín wrote about in the letter.

"Papeles."

He'd written Estela, worried about his papers, not knowing what to do. Much later, when I was old enough to understand, he told me it was disorienting to have a few sheets of off-white paper be so determinant in our lives. "I might be seeing you really soon," he'd written.

To "have papers" or "not have papers" was something frequently discussed and central in my household. From the time I was very young, thinking about our situation as one of papers helped me understand something of the arbitrariness of the whole thing. I remember asking a young blonde girl I had a crush on early in elementary school about her papers, and she not knowing what I was talking about. It was the first time I realized some people didn't even know they had papers, and that absence of knowledge for people like her was something new I learned about *my* situation.

Not having these documents but needing them reveals a quality of contemporary American life that many people don't have to see. Things as banal as paperwork, based on arbitrarily selected dates, are used to administer suffering. To not have papers is to be marked as someone who is banned. And to be banned in this way is to be made the walking, breathing expression of sovereignty. You prove that "America" exists. You prove that a quality called "American" exists by being made to represent what it is not. To some, we are the chiseled-away material in relief.

Once after a shift at the restaurant I asked Octavio to describe the feeling of driving his green Geo without a driver's license. He said he tried not to think about it but that it doesn't work that way. He told me there's always something in the back of his head that understands the precariousness of each passing moment, that sometimes it's not something one actively thinks about, but it's still there, like a pain "en el pinche culo." I felt guilty whenever he drove me home. I even tried to avoid him when we had shifts together so he wouldn't, but he always insisted. That night, when we were nearing my apartment, he took a right when he was supposed to make a left. He explained that this was because his left blinker wasn't working so he was trying to only turn right. He knew if he got pulled over he would be at the mercy of the individual police officer. "Chicago es okay," he said. He explained he even got pulled over once and was let go with a warning, but one of his friends, a guy who used to collect scrap metal in a pickup truck, got caught up while he was out collecting one day. He was in an alley and he T-boned a woman in a white BMW pulling out of her garage. They took him in, and his wife and kids didn't know what happened until a few days later when he was already in the process of being removed.

"Are you a US citizen?"

The question can result in being taken away on the spot. No going home, even if you have something slow-cooking on the stove, a cat, or even children. If you have kids and you're taken in, the ACLU recommends that you "call a friend or family member as soon as possible so that a responsible adult will be able to take care of them," because otherwise their fates are open-ended questions with only a horrible range of possibilities. But sometimes people aren't permitted a phone call, and what if you have no one to call? Despite federal assertions that immigration enforcement prioritizes serious threats to public safety and national security, the *New York Times* reported in April 2014 that "since President Obama took office, two-thirds of the nearly two million deportation cases involve people who had committed minor infractions, including traffic violations, or had no criminal record at all." In fact, the article shows not only that the largest increases were in deportations of undocumented immigrants, often whose most serious offense was a traffic violation, but that the cases more than quadrupled from 43,000 during George W. Bush's last half-decade in office to 193,000 during a five-year span in the Obama administration.

Yoli couldn't sleep on the night of May 4, 1988. She says she didn't sleep the previous evening, the night of my third birthday, either. Her mind was fixed on a drip coming from a faucet, maybe in the kitchen, maybe in the bathroom, and she spent the night between the evenly spaced intervals of sound until the sun came up. At the same time, Martín lay next to her perfectly still, his eyes closed, also unable to rest. Each thought the other was sleeping, or perhaps they didn't care what the other was doing. Both spent the night turning an impossible question over and over in their minds: *What are we going to do?*

Midnight on May 4 was the deadline for the major phase of the Immigration Reform and Control Act of 1986 (IRCA), and in order to qualify for relief one had to be able to prove continuous residence in the United States since January 1, 1982. We had no way of doing that. Midnight came and went, and Yoli says when she got out of bed the following morning, everything felt pointless in a way that made her feel light. She wanted to smoke a cigarette, something she hadn't done since she was a girl when she would steal butts from her father's ashtray and smoke the remainder when they sent her to the store. Martín said he felt like he had failed us, and he doesn't think he would have been able to get out of bed if not for the fact that he had to go to work or we wouldn't eat.

Under this main provision, 1.7 million people received temporary residence if they paid a $185 fee and were of "good moral character." Some would then be able to apply for permanent residence after eighteen months, if they spoke English. The bill included provisions for tightening border security with new technology, and penalties for employers who hired undocumented workers, but by the time it became law, business interests (like California fruit and vegetable growers, who were the biggest exploiters of undocumented migrant labor) had effectively lobbied to declaw employer sanctions. Not surprising, since Reagan was the former Republican governor of California.

The months following the deadline held a peculiar feeling for Yoli. She saw two frozen crows on two separate occasions in February and took it as a bad omen. One of them appeared to have frozen while standing under a tree, and it remained stiff, on its side. The image disturbed her: from time to time she brings it up, never in context, just the image of the crow having frozen alive, perhaps on its feet. She said she felt as though she couldn't breathe in enough, like time during that stretch of days felt like waiting, except she didn't know for what. At moments she felt resigned, and this brought calm. She says she spent a lot of time staring at the door, daydreaming about what it would look like when someone came through it. In other moments she felt a panic she'd felt when she was a girl and knew something bad was coming. Each time the phone rang it triggered muscle spasms under her diaphragm, and she could feel a fluttering that made it difficult to breathe. This was before caller ID, and we didn't have an answering machine, so sometimes it would ring and ring and it wouldn't stop, so she would pick me up and take me to the park. Neither of them ever said anything about it to each other, they didn't want to acknowledge it, but in the mornings when Martín left for work there was a sharp moment in which they looked at one another and felt the abhorrent possibility each time he walked out the door.

Yoli takes a bite of her concha, and then there's a knock at the door. She inhales some of the white crumbs and almost chokes.

"Ha de ser tu pinche padre," she says.

When I open the door he's standing there holding a foot-long plaster statue of the archangel Michael crushing Lucifer's head under his foot.

"What the fuck is that?" I ask.

He chuckles.

"An old lady from work gave it to me," he responds.

It's one thirty in the afternoon and he's home from work already because he's been there since 4 a.m. Whenever I visit and stay at my parents' house I hear him leave for work right around the time I go to sleep. When certain people ask what he does, I tell them, and there's an awkward pause, and then they avert their eyes. A lot of times the answer is a conversation ender. When it's not, the person to whom I've said it carries on talking hurriedly, without acknowledging it. Once, when I told an affluent white guy I was acquainted with that my father worked at an industrial food production plant, he awkwardly blurted out something like, "but he's, like, a manager, right?" I extended his discomfort as long as I could before answering. "He's a shift manager." It means he stands in a giant refrigerated warehouse with no windows overseeing the production of prepared food items for various retailers. Everything is done on various assembly lines, and the workers on his lines are contracted and subcontracted labor.

He takes off his boots and sits down on the couch. Yoli hands me a single sheet of paper from the box and tells me to show it to him. It's a photocopy of a handwritten flyer with a heading that reads "Special Agricultural Workers."

"Holy shit," he says when he sees it.

He explains that one day he was walking to work after getting off the train, and a young kid—maybe eighteen or nineteen—standing on a street corner handed a flyer to him, that he never used to take flyers or things people tried to hand him but that for some reason he took that one. "You have until Nov. 30, 1988 to file! Your application must be complete, and submitted with all the required documentation." That's how he found out there was another deadline and another way to qualify for the IRCA. Farmhands were eligible if they had some way of proving they'd worked harvesting vegetables, fruits, or any other perishable crops for at least ninety days during a one-year period that ended May 1, 1986.

"Around that time," he says, "estaba de la puta madre."

It felt to Martín and Yoli as though they lived teetering on a precipice. "I think we might be seeing each other really soon," he'd written his mother. He said that la migra maintained a "presence" in Chicago, both before and after the law passed. "It didn't feel like they were trying to round everyone up, or shut everything down for real. You know? They'd send two or three agents here, two or three agents there."

One morning, Nacho, a guy he worked with, warned him he'd seen two agents in olive green uniforms at the Milwaukee and Western bus stop taking a few paisas away in cuffs. It really spooked him because that was just four or five blocks from our house, and he took the Western blue line. He walked by that spot every morning on his way to work. Another time a friend told him about his brother who worked in a factory that got raided. They kicked in the doors and stormed in with guns drawn, and the brother couldn't run anywhere because they had the place surrounded, so he climbed inside a big plastic drum and stayed crouched for five or six hours until everything was quiet. He waited another two for good measure, and he would have waited longer but his knees felt like they were going to pop. When he climbed out, the huge production room was empty. He'd never seen the lines still, without workers on them. They'd taken around fifty people. A constellation of hairnets and pairs of orange earplugs connected by blue vinyl string were strewn across the production floor.

Martín fit the incredibly narrow criteria and was granted temporary residence.

"I always try to remember what the kid who gave me the flier looked like, but I can't. I can't even remember if he was white or black or a *paisa* or what. I think he was wearing a red jacket or maybe black—I don't know."

He says he felt a second of relief that was drowned out by the fact that Yoli and I didn't qualify. It's estimated that around 1.3 million people applied under the agricultural worker criteria, so in total around three million of the estimated five million undocumented individuals living in the United States suddenly had temporary status. Employer sanctions were gutted, but the raids and periodic snatching of people off the street continued. The final version of the law meant the only thing employers had to do to avoid culpability was make sure their employees' paperwork "reasonably appears on its face to be genuine," which meant the Justice Department would only be able to prosecute if they could prove that employers were hiring undocumented workers *intentionally.* Other times industries like landscaping, construction, factory work, and agriculture maneuvered around any liability whatsoever by using contracted and subcontracted labor.

On November 6, 1986, upon signing the IRCA, Ronald Reagan released a statement in which he outlined his reasons for signing the bill into law. Part of it reads:

> In 1981 this administration asked the Congress to pass a comprehensive legislative package, including employer sanctions, other measures to increase enforcement of the immigration laws, and legalization. The act provides these three essential components. The employer sanctions program is the keystone and major element. It will remove the incentive for illegal immigration by eliminating the job opportunities, which draw illegal aliens here. We have consistently supported a legalization program, which is both generous to the alien and fair to the countless thousands of people throughout the world who seek legally to come to America. The legalization provisions in this act will go far to improve the lives of a class of individuals who now must hide in the shadows, without access to many of the benefits of a free and open society. Very soon many of these men and women will be able to step into the sunlight and, ultimately, if they choose, they may become Americans.

We now know these words were coming from a president whose eight years in office were among the bloodiest in the

history of the Western Hemisphere. His administration continued the long-standing US tradition of making incursions
into the affairs of Latin American countries, and since this
was the Cold War it was in the name of anticommunism.
In Guatemala, Reagan provided the right-wing government
with military and economic support despite the State Department and White House being apprised of the ongoing
violence under the leadership of Ríos Montt. In 1982 the US
embassy in Guatemala sent cables to Washington right after a massacre in the Ixtil village of Sacuchum. One of the
cables specified, "Reports of torture and strangulation (and
possible incidents of rape) [suggest] the modus operandi of
the extreme right." As these cables came in, the US State
Department continued publicly asserting that it could not
"definitively attribute the killing to one group or another"
and that the Guatemalan military was "taking care to protect innocent bystanders." In classified memos from the very
same months, Deputy Assistant Secretary of State Stephen
Bosworth reported that "the military continues to engage in
massacres of civilians in the countryside" and said his department had recently received a "well-founded allegation of a
large-scale killing of Indian men, women and children in a
remote area by the army."

Many who survived were interned in "model villages" that
were nothing more than detention camps supplied by the
US Agency for International Development (USAID). After the period of open massacres ended, targeted assassina-
tions by death squads with ties to the Central Intelligence
Agency continued to torture and kill alleged dissidents into
the nineties. A truth commission report published in 1999,
titled "Guatemala: Memory of Silence," estimated that two
hundred thousand people were killed or disappeared and
that 93 percent of the human rights violations and acts of
violence registered by the commission were "attributable to
actions by the State." The commission also found that "the

Army's perception of Mayan communities" played a part in the "aggressive racist component of extreme cruelty that led to the extermination en masse, of defenceless Mayan communities." The US-backed Guatemalan army perpetrated

> acts such as the killing of defenceless children, often by beating them against walls . . . throwing them alive into pits where the corpses of adults were later thrown; the amputation of limbs; the impaling of victims; the killing of persons by covering them in petrol and burning them alive; the extraction, in the presence of others, of the viscera of victims who were still alive; the confinement of people who had been mortally tortured, in agony for days; the opening of the wombs of pregnant women, and other similarly atrocious acts.

Reagan supported similarly atrocious conflicts in El Salvador and, most famously, Nicaragua during his presidency.

Although it's impossible to say with certainty what the motivations were for legislators and the president in passing the IRCA, I feel confident thinking it had nothing to do with reducing immigration, improving lives, or helping people "step into the sunlight." What it did do was allow the United States to reset a game board by regularizing the immigration status of the people who were already here, while leaving the policies that had made them "illegal" to begin with in place for the next wave of immigrants, so that they too would be inscribed with the same vulnerabilities.

Maybe it had something to do with Mexico's strategic place in Latin America during the Cold War. It feels as though part of my reality—and Martín's and Yoli's realities—will always remain arbitrary and unintelligible. I have a very clear memory of something that happened during the mid-1990s when my dad and I were watching TV. The local news broadcast came on. It played a clip of Ronald Reagan in Hollywood wearing a cowboy hat, putting a saddle on a

horse, and then a clip of President Reagan standing at a po-
dium in front of the Brandenburg Gate, telling Gorbachev
to "tear down that wall." The anchor announced that Reagan
had just been diagnosed with Alzheimer's, and I knew what
that was because one of our neighbors, an old Polish lady,
suffered from it, and Yoli had explained what it meant. Martín said something like "Que se lo carge la chingada" and
turned off the TV. I think I remember it still because my
dad badmouthing someone suffering such misfortune wasn't
something I'd heard or thought I would ever hear. It was a
long while before I understood.

CHAPTER 3

Biometrics

This morning my eyes are slits and I'm grumbling to Ariel, my friend in the passenger seat, about these appointments being so sudden. A week earlier I'd received a certified letter with the Department of Homeland Security seal on it—a blue eagle holding an olive branch in one talon and thirteen arrows in the other. It was a summons to have my biometrics captured, to have my fingerprints cleared by the FBI, one step closer to being naturalized. Ariel offered to come along to keep me from falling asleep at the wheel and crashing the car I borrowed. We'd also half-joked that her whiteness would keep us both safe.

My appointment: February 14, 2011. 210 Walnut Street. 1 p.m. Des Moines, Iowa.

Shards of sunlight have just started creeping over the long hills along I-80 West. We made sure to leave early enough to make it on time in the event of a flat tire or some other incident. Ariel snaps photos of me driving.

"So you'll remember."

She snaps another one, squinting behind the viewfinder. "Are you excited?"

I watch the sunrise tremble in the rearview. It takes me a moment to answer.

"Not really."

45

It takes another moment to work out that "not really" is, in fact, precisely true.

When I moved out of my parents' house a few years back, my mom told me to make sure to report to Homeland Security.

"To *what?*"

"Homeland Security. En el Internet."

She explained that as "lawful permanent residents" we had to report to the US Citizenship and Immigration Service—one of seven agencies that comprise the Department of Homeland Security—within ten days of moving.

"Or what?"

She shrugs.

"Pues quién sabe."

Valentine's Day. Along I-80, the corn and soy have long been harvested, the landscape is topped with husks and wisps of snow. What's left is the gray geometry of agribusiness. Talk radio has been tranquilizing me with a voice at a volume so low that it no longer carries words, only textures. I feel like I'm gliding on the muted surface of a Luc Tuymans painting: colors one would expect from a drowned corpse, images stripped of their context and mediated into blasé obscurity. The monstrous actuality of the landscape concealed by its absolute banality.

In these conditions, it's hard to remain aware that I'm driving, that there's a passenger in the seat next to me. I zone out, and my eyes trace a hawk detaching from a wire. It crosses in front of the car, and as I follow it my gaze becomes fixed on my hand on the steering wheel and then on the valley between my index and middle knuckle. I sink into a memory of a front yard when I was eleven. I was meeting a friend in front of his house, by his grandfather's flagpole and the three-story evergreen that bent under its own weight.

For a moment everything was still, and then the unmistakable buzz of some kind of projectile cut through the air incredibly close to my face. A boy yelled something too suddenly for me to understand. My eyes searched for the source and came to two small faces in the third-story window: my friend crouching and another boy giggling. Another rush of air. This one hit between the knuckles of my hand covering my face, producing a sharp burning. I ran and didn't stop until I reached the end of the next block, where I finally registered that they'd been screaming "Border Patrol!" and shooting at me with a BB gun.

Today it's Valentine's Day, and even though I'm in the process of being—at least nominally—included as a full member of US society, these points of contact with the Department of Homeland Security don't feel like love. *What do I have to do with the FBI?* Ariel is saying something. I glance at her face and then back at the road, but all I can think about is the vast, amorphous power we're moving toward. My mind can't settle on a representation because the nature of this power seems as mysterious, complex, and ever-changing as an ecological system or metabolism. I glance at Ariel's moving lips and at the white salt spots on the windshield. My mind cycles through images of power: the Pentagon, a baroque black-and-white etching of a scaffold, a pane of glass with thousands of fractures moving in all directions, with no discernable origin. *Who exactly will be looking at my fingerprints? Where will this information go?*

We pull off the highway.

Downtown Des Moines is one of those North American metropolises absent of pedestrians, all sharp lines and dead angles. A few homeless men stand in a park smoking.

Ariel snaps a photo of me making a stupid face, holding the immigration document in one hand, and giving a thumbs-up with the other. Behind me, across the street, the federal building fills the rest of the photograph with its all-glass exterior. She snaps another: me kissing the iron federal seal emerging from the concrete wall, my lips hovering inches from the thirteen arrowheads in the eagle's talons. This year, the immigration document is my only valentine, and it feels like I'm trapped in an abusive relationship with a sociopath. My whereabouts, purchases, and behaviors must be known. My associations must be scrutinized, my intentions justified.

Just inside the revolving doors are two armed guards who look bored but perk up the second Ariel and I enter the building. We're probably the first people they've seen in hours. The one in front of the walk-through metal detector is shaped like a sweet potato. He furrows his brow.

"Purse on the belt."

All business. He doesn't even crack a smile for Ariel—a tall, lean girl—on Valentine's Day. Her purse disappears into the X-ray machine. The smaller guard looks at his screen, scrunching the bridge of his nose, tracing contours, trying to detect any deviation. Nothing. She meets it on the other side.

I'd failed to imagine this machine, these two guards. I've been standing in place, feeling the need to be perfectly still, suddenly aware of my entire body's surface. My attempt to take mental inventory of my backpack is condensing tension into beads of sweat on my forehead and upper lip. I know there's nothing of concern in my bag, but I have a shoddy memory, and there are so many small pockets tucked away.

"Bag on the belt."

This time he's talking to me, and there's nothing to do at this point but put the bag on the belt. We're both fixed in our roles, transacting in suspicion, guilt, and fear. I feel observed, not only by the soft-faced guard standing in front of me, but also by the juridical presence in the walls.

Ariel smiles from the other side.

My bag disappears, and the guard behind the machine scrunches his nose again. I can't tell if he's looking harder, scrunching more for me than for Ariel. The belt stops. He calls for the other guard, who's been standing in front of me, breathing heavily, staring at my face. They look at the screen, take turns pointing, and murmur to each other.

Ariel stands on the other side waiting, and I expel a nervous chuckle like the ones that erupt at funerals for no apparent reason. They've reversed my bag out of the X-ray machine. The bigger of the two guards pats and squeezes it, furrows his brow, and looks at me like I've done something wrong.

"What's in this bag?"

Ariel is no longer smiling.

"Uh, books."

His job is to suspect and intimidate. I have no idea whether or not this has anything to do with the fact that I'm brown, but he's staring at my face, and I imagine he sees me as I see him, which is to say in the most reductive and obvious way. There's no opportunity for meaningful communication, or any communication really, just the reception of narrow data with which to fix a type.

What type does this man think I am?

In a piss dive in Dallas a few years back, a big, white biker bought me a drink and showed me the World War I trench knife he carried strapped to his boot.

"My grandpappy's."

Each of his thick, knotted fingers filled the individual holes of the knuckle grips. He made a fist, and his hand became a spiked weapon pointed at my gut.

"Skull crusher." Holding the eleven-inch knife upright, he tapped the brass-spiked handle against his wooden stool.

"This," he said, fingering the spiked pommel, "this'll crack you open."

His voice crackled like campfire and indicated a certain kind of life. I could feel that the absolute wrong thing to do was to get up and walk away. I could feel that the only thing to do was order both of us another round, this time a double, and sit there until we reached a kind of end.

"That is an excellent knife."

I said it casually. I had to demonstrate that this was not the first time a drunk had shown me his knife, or if it was, that I had led the kind of life that would render me unmoved. I *was* unmoved—not because it wasn't terrifying, but because I'd been around violence before, and because I had confidence that if I drank fast, faster than he did, I'd be fine, and because at that juncture in life I was too tired to care very much about my well-being. I ordered round after round of Wild Turkey, ordered a beer in a bottle, and placed it where I could swat it into his face if I had to.

Eventually he slid the knife back into his boot.

"Now let me ask you one question." His tone shifted and he looked at my face excitedly, like a kid trying to contain his laughter as he's about to tell a joke. Motörhead's "Killed by Death" was blaring on the jukebox, so he leaned in and put his arm around my shoulders so I could hear him. I felt his hot breath on my earlobe. He smelled good—like tobacco, exhaust, and whiskey.

"Are you a sand nigger or a spic?"

He stared at my face, and I stared at his. Deep creases that looked like scars or a river's tributaries lined his features. Half of his long white beard was tucked into his shirt. He looked like an old fighting dog that had never managed to die. *Now, right now, something is going to happen,* I thought, gripping my bottle of beer and positioning it on the bar adjacent to him so that I could pivot off my stool and smash it into his face, but he erupted with laughter that quickly broke into a wet hacking fit. He slapped me on the back, laughing, turning red in the face. I loosened my grip on the bottle.

I started laughing too because the tension had broken. I slid him my beer.

"Take a drink, man, for God's sake."

His wet gurgling fit paired well with Lemmy Kilmister's voice and the shiny velvet Elvis that stared at us from across the room. He chugged the entire beer, and we went outside for a smoke. The broad street was completely abandoned, and as we sucked down our cigarettes a couple of coyotes flashed across the road in the distance under the streetlights.

"So which is it?"

The guards at the metal detector have zeroed in on a specific item. One of them is squeezing the main compartment of my bag.

"What's this?"

"I have no idea. You can just open it and take a look."

The suggestion seems to agitate him. He continues squeezing and shifting the item around. I try to read his face for any inclination of what he might be thinking, but it's no use. I've noticed that for some time now I've been feeling increasingly jumpy about the way people look at me, particularly white people. I'm not sure if it's because I've gotten older and am more aware of the ways I'm perceived because of my appearance, or if people *have* been looking at me differently because of the xenophobic nature of our cultural moment. This process has exacerbated my sensitivity, though, because it's served as an unpleasant reminder that in the eyes of the US government I'm only just "earning" my place here. And while I understand that I'm increasingly fortunate to be moving in this direction, it feels like I'm accepting terms that have been decided for me, accepting the notion that up until now I have been categorically different, and that this difference is a legitimate reason to be subject to a different, more punitive existence.

Maybe right now the guards are just having fun because I present something to do, a reason to move their legs, a situation to animate their atrophied sense of purpose. They must get bored being the keepers of these small and desolate gates, having to see the same federal employees, delivery workers, and mail carriers every day. Strangers become familiar strangers by sheer force of repetition and proximity, and there is a distance that is closed so that a new stranger is recognizable as unrecognizable.

After more staring, some whispering among themselves, and a few more cautious pats, one of the guards has me open the bag and pull out the suspicious item: a Tupperware container full of grapes.

There are two barcodes on my valentine. My name appears in all caps without the proper marks: JOSE MARTIN ORDUNA. I can't remember whether I included them in my original application. I'm not sure if I included my mother's surname or whether this is necessary. I'm not sure that I haven't been slightly changing my name with each official document, leaving a trail of abandoned aliases with shifting pasts, credit reports, and medical histories. I've never known what my full name actually is, and what I'm supposed to write on any given line. Usually there isn't enough space to include what my mother tells me my name is: José Martín Orduña Gonzalez.

I do know that the inconsistencies have prevented me from boarding airplanes. The sight of a bearded brown man speaking English too perfectly, with a driver's license that reads JOSE M ORDUNA, a green Mexican passport that reads JOSÉ MARTIN ORDUÑA GONZALEZ, and a boarding pass that reads JOSE MARTIN ORDUNA is enough to cause some trouble.

The very top of the valentine reads "Department of Homeland Security." Underneath that: "US Citizenship and Immigration Services." Below that, "THE UNITED STATES OF AMERICA" stretches the width of the page in the proprietary font found on US currency. The fat letters sit heavily and seem immovable and permanent, just like the idea of money itself. The page even seems to be made of a similar material as dollar bills. It's some kind of counterfeit-proof paper with different colored fibers worked into the page. It immediately communicates its authority, an authority it has granted itself through force and violence, and it strikes me how such a strong signal can be communicated on something as insubstantial as a single sheet of paper.

In the middle of the page, the arm of Lady Liberty ghosts behind the words "ALIEN," "CENTER," and "ABAN-DONED." There is a reminder to bring my Alien Registration Card.

When I was ten my dad gave me my first wallet—it was green, with the Teenage Mutant Ninja Turtles on the outside. Then he handed me my identification card, my first green card, which was actually pink. He said we'd gotten it when we'd gone to Juárez but that he didn't think I was ready to carry it then. I remembered we'd gone very suddenly and that I missed my third-grade class trip to an amusement park, that a man I'd never seen showed up at our door in Chicago, and that my dad let him into our house. The next day we were on a Greyhound bus that took three days to get to El Paso, Texas, and then we immediately took a cab across a bridge into Juárez. We stayed in a strip mall motel where the television in the next room played straight through the night. I remember lying awake with my eyes open, watching my dad go to the window to peer out through the blinds several times and also going to the door to stand silently in the darkness listening. He got up at four o'clock to hold a place in a line across the road, and later that morning I watched my mom fix me breakfast with a mini cereal box that was on the dresser, powdered milk she'd gotten at a gas station, and a bottle of water. I remember being enthralled by the powdered milk.

At age ten I looked at my new card. Just above my three-quarter-angle bust was a term I hadn't known: "RESIDENT ALIEN."

"Ha," I laughed. "I'm an alien."

I remember my dad staring back at me with a grim look, the one he used to shoot me when he needed me to know something serious was happening. I remember him telling me I was a man now, despite my crooked flattop and wiry frame.

"A man never leaves home without his wallet."

Then he asked if I remembered Jorge.

"Who?"

"Jorge, the fat guy with a limp that used to work with me at the hotel."

Yes. I'd seen him hobbling around after a soccer ball at one of the rare social gatherings my father had time off work for.

"Jorge didn't have his green card with him."

I'd gotten distracted by Michelangelo's orange mask, so he gently raised my head with his fingers.

"He's gone now."

I didn't really understand. I'd never really understood what it meant that we lived in Chicago but had come from Mexico because it was never explained to me in explicit terms. Like most children I took things as they came, as-similating almost everything into my milieu and assuming it was all normal. I did recognize that this thing he'd given me meant something important, though, because it came with my own wallet, which was an accessory I'd seen all my uncles, my dad, and my friends' dads handling. It's where they kept the things that tied them to the adult world of obligations, transactions, and identifications. I remember thinking it would be impossible to keep track of this object at all times, but that's exactly what I did.

My dad smiled at me, patted me on the head, and told me to put it in my pocket.

"Don't lose it."

Years later, my new green card, this one actually green, is in my wallet as I enter the Department of Homeland Security office. It says "PERMANENT RESIDENT CARD" at the top, a slightly nicer iteration to carry around. It displays the Department of Homeland Security seal, not the Department of Justice seal, because the "War on Terror" birthed this hungry new entity that absorbed and restructured twenty-two federal agencies. The US government reacted to the events of 9/11 by creating a top-secret architecture whose growth was so unmitigated that it's still impossible to know how much it costs to operate, how many people it includes, and exactly how many programs fall under its rubric. Another result was the increased privatization of counterterrorism, homeland security, and intelligence. In 2004, Accenture, an offshore "global management consulting, technology services and outsourcing company," became the well-paid brain behind US-VISIT, the United States Visitor and Immigrant Status Indicator Technology program. According to the DHS website,

> US-VISIT systems provide identity verification and analysis services and data-sharing capabilities to multiple stakeholders, including the Departments of Justice, Defense, and State; DHS components; the Intelligence Community; State and local law enforcement agencies; and a growing list of foreign government partners.

In 2013 the program was renamed the Office of Biometric Identity Management (OBIM), but its mission will remain essentially the same: to capture the unique human body characteristics of as many people as possible, link it to their biographical information, and make it easily accessible to "stakeholders." By now the OBIM database, the Automated Biometric Identification System (IDENT), must circulate millions if not hundreds of millions of biometric identities, and the goal is to "accommodate the storage, extractions, and matching of new modalities, such as face and iris, and to integrate biographic and biometric data more effectively."

There is no doubt that IDENT has helped the Obama administration reach record-breaking deportation figures year after year.

The juridical presence in the walls.

Ariel is walking next to me into the mostly empty office. Every time she smiles at me I feel obligated to smile back, which is a good distraction from what it is I'm actually feeling. She insists I take notes in one of my pocket notebooks.

"So you'll remember."

I tell her this is something I am sure to never forget.

She makes a note-taking gesture, so I reach into the inside pocket of my trench coat and open to a blank page. I scatter mostly unusable observations in no particular order.

Two days before my appointment I ran into my Minnesota friend, Robert Plantenberg.

"That," he pointed at my upper lip, "is a moustache of some consequence."

He's white, six foot one, and has an innocuous build. He wears glasses. He has male pattern baldness I can only describe as handsome, and a robust brown beard that's perfectly symmetrical. He is wearing what he calls his Bob suit, a suit I've come to understand grants him authority or invisibility, depending on what's necessary at the time, and gives him access to all kinds of things that are off limits to others. It allows him the luxury of walking around unencumbered by others' perceptions of him and leaves him free of having to calculate what those might be in order to sustain his very life. His exterior is one of the templates for what we think of as an American. Bob is astute, so he's perfectly aware that his Bob suit gives him power, which is why I think he always offers to drive whenever we hang out. Over the course of our relationship he's relayed a few stories about times when he calmly talked his way out of hairy situations that I'm sure would have turned out very differently for me.

Bob and I also frequent a taco place where I recently pointed out something that I noticed a while back: when I wear a mustache, paisas will greet me in Spanish, but when I have a full beard or am cleanly shaven they usually wait for me to say something first or they'll begin in English. I first observed this in high school, during summer breaks, when I started making forays into growing facial hair. Besides the different greetings I'd receive from other Latin Americans, I noticed white girls paid less attention to me. In stores, it seemed white people would ask me where things were more frequently, and when I told them I wasn't an employee they'd either look very surprised, somewhat amused, or intensely embarrassed. The strangest thing, though, was some white people seemed to lose the ability to see me at all, as though I held no physical space in a room, as though I had no materiality with which to displace air or cast shadows.

"Bob, do you think I should shave this moustache before my appointment?"

"Yes."

Ariel is not supposed to be here, according to my valentine. "WARNING! Due to limited seating availability in our lobby areas, only persons who are necessary to assist with transportation or completing the fingerprint worksheet should accompany you." I look up from my notebook and there are two women who might be African sitting a few seats away, next to each other. I don't think they're here together because one is wearing a solid purple head wrap that's tightly twisted around her head, while the other woman's is shiny and voluminous, and looks like a *gele*. The room we're in looks like it could fit hundreds comfortably, but there are only five people in here including Ariel. One of the women smiles warmly at me, and nods her head, which I take to mean she's happy for me—happy I've made it here to this room—because she knows the value of the papers dispensed through this office. But it feels Faustian to voluntarily become an "American" in this historical moment, and it feels funny to be relieved about no longer being deportable by the same state that can still easily kill me "legally" and with absolute impunity.

I feel stuck in the eternal return of the circumstances into which I was born. The arbitrariness of where I came into being is reified by and as institutions, which themselves are in the process of becoming more immaterial, more abstract through secrecy and the yet unknowable consequences of emerging technology. The Department of Homeland Security works with countless private partners with little oversight. They have numbers they'd like to meet, and the details are left to the subcontractors. Iris scans, enhanced facial recognition tracking, full hand geometry. But who exactly will have access to the biometric data of hundreds of millions of people, now and in the future? How did something like IDENT come online without even the semblance of informed consent?

The operational paradigm is broad interoperability, which means the free exchange of information and services between diverse government systems. It means fusion centers within local police precincts that aggregate mass amounts of data from a variety of public- and private-sector sources operating under the auspices of national security. In 2008 the Los Angeles Police Department began monitoring individuals' everyday activities. They came up with a list of sixty-five behaviors, including using binoculars, attempting to take measurements, taking pictures or video footage "with no apparent aesthetic value," drawing diagrams, abandoning a vehicle, taking notes, and espousing extremist views, which "could indicate activity or intentions related to either foreign or domestic terrorism." They were able to do this because the Department of Justice did away with federal regulations that governed criminal intelligence databases and expanded what kinds of information can be collected by local law enforcement and with whom it can be shared. This Suspicious Activity Report (SAR) program has since gone nationwide, which means that in addition to the mass information-gathering and surveillance that happens online, information about noncriminal activity is also being gathered offline in cities and towns all over the United States. A robust and steady stream of this information constantly flows into federal intelligence databases. The mission is to record, upload, and be able to extract exploitable meaning from everything; to fully capitalize on our cultural tendency and technological ability to force everything that will ever be thought through a recordable medium; to fill every crevice with a camera's gaze, an accessible microphone; to comprehensively map human relations in real time; to make predictions that allow more comprehensive, broader management over life; and to make all of this available to a chosen operator from a single searchable database accessible from any laptop or mobile device.

I look down and notice I haven't filled out the form sitting in my lap. It asks for my alien number so I retrieve my green card. The letter "A" followed by nine digits. Tolstoy wrote in his private diaries that there are proper names, real names, names of things, animals and people, which evoke the way of life better than a description of the thing itself. The alien number constitutes one of my names in the system, lets the analyst know what my restrictions in movement and labor are, what my ports of entry and exit have been, and may be connected to what kind of trouble I've been getting into, if any. In the system, I am a collection of linked information filed under the category of Alien. When these points of data become aggregated and disseminated among systems that determine humans' lives, they allow for the expulsion and management of populations along lines of demarcation forged and maintained through violence. They allow for laws that inscribe themselves preemptively on the bodies and souls of people, laws that can act upon them from a great distance always exerting pressures that never let up. They allow for the displacement and expulsion of millions of individuals who are all members of families and communities. In many paradigms of social justice, people fight to be seen, named, and recognized, but in light of these systems of mass surveillance it seems we need to reclaim anonymity, unrecognizability, the right to be left alone.

I have no idea where *I* am in this relation between the signifier and the signified.

It feels like I'm betraying myself when I write the number on the line. I do it in bad faith.

This is my official identification, composed of narrow points of data that are reassembled in permutations to serve others' purposes. These identities refer to me, a reference that others own. These official permutations become my virtual selves, selves that have so little to do with me and yet contain information essential to my lived experience, selves that become unrecognizable to me—versions alleged to be me trapped to endlessly drag themselves along a razor's edge of perpetually self-replicating virtual borders. They signal *what* I am because these systems can't collect *who* I am.

It feels like a sick love affair: a faceless power needing to know my every move, utterance, thought, and behavior even though there's no reason for me to be under observation or suspicion. It seems my valentine finds me threatening, which reveals more about my valentine than it does about me.

I hand in the form, and a portly woman with a stern face

comes around the corner. She provides an obligatory smile. She positions me in front of a white backdrop and raises a digital camera in front of my face.

"Smile, darling."

We walk to what looks like a copy machine except it's bigger than I am. The woman speaks warmly to me. She puts on a pair of latex gloves, takes my hand, and puts each of my digits on a clear glass grid individually, then together, and then it's over. She hands me an alcohol wipe and tells me I'll be receiving another notice as soon as the FBI clears me.

"That's it?"

"That's it."

Ariel: "That's it?"

"That's it."

I look at my watch. "Tasty Tacos?"

My friend Chelsea, a native of Des Moines, made me promise that after the capturing of my biometric data, Ariel and I would eat at Tasty Tacos. She smiled facetiously, displaying her prominent incisors when I agreed.

"Starting with virtually nothing, we have taken a family recipe and given people across the country an opportunity to sample our one-of-a-kind flour taco." In 1961, the Mosqueda family didn't imagine they'd own five profitable "fast serve restaurants." Ariel and I can't stop smiling at this mongrel food establishment: Formica diner booths and tables; an old-school slide-lettering menu above the cash register that's faded yellow and spattered with some kind of dried red sauce; a fat, mustachioed man with a long, braided ponytail; a group of three construction workers—one black, one white, one brown—all wearing tan Carhartt jackets. A family of three—a morbidly obese white woman whose lower stomach is dangerously wedged under the table, her racially ambiguous partner, and their even more racially ambiguous child who's going to town on two corn dogs.

I look at my red tray, with one hard-shell chicken taco—

chicken that feels, between my teeth, to have been boiled—
one shriveled corn dog that tastes thawed from a long deep
freeze, and one small cola in a disposable cup with the restaurant's logo: a young Mexican boy wearing a sombrero
with a sarape slung over his left shoulder, his hands extended,
in the small reverie of being a man. He exclaims, "Nada Es
Imposible!"

CHAPTER 4

La Soledad de Octavio

To live is to be separated from what we were
in order to approach what we are going to be
in the mysterious future.

—*Octavio Paz*, The Labyrinth of Solitude

"Chhhht, cabrón." Octavio swats at my head because we're three cans of Tecate in, and I've forgotten to speak quietly again. He lives in a small, single-family home with his wife, her mother, his brother-in-law, his brother-in-law's wife, their infant son, and his wife's widowed cousin. One overweight Yorkie named Cookie yips incessantly while looking out the window, and another one, an emaciated, seventeen-year-old male named Coco, bumbles about in a diaper, drooling, until he finds himself in a corner and freezes, at which point someone turns him around so he can get stuck in another corner. In a small office past the kitchen, an African grey parrot sleeps standing on his perch.

I'm home for the weekend, visiting from graduate school in Iowa, which feels like being stuck in a tiny aquarium that never gets cleaned. The displeasure of being perpetually surrounded by graduate students and academics gets to be unbearable, and cooking meals for one and eating them in a silent apartment shaves away at the psyche. I've recently taken to setting my laptop across from me while eating meals and playing a YouTube video that simulates dinner conversation with another human. I've gone so far as to set two place settings, one for me and one for the laptop. I serve my food, sit down, and hit play, and for twenty minutes the cleavage and lower face of a young woman with an English accent makes noises and produces brief interjections that make it seem like I'm a charming and intelligent conversationalist. The prerecorded video tells me how great I look, how it looks like I've lost weight, how my taste in clothing is perfect. The woman's voice is soft, eliciting a vaguely sexual tingle in my ears and scalp.

After about a week of eating meals like this, I decide it would be best to go home.

Everyone's asleep at Octavio's house except the two of us and Cookie, who's staring out the window at a group of hipsters drinking beer in the park. Earlier that day I'd texted Octavio a picture of a frozen Iowan cornfield from the Megabus.

My text read, "La soledad es el hecho más profundo de la condición humana."

"No mames guey, tan chidas las flores. Salgo a las doce. Doble," he'd responded.

He usually works six dobles a week: a lunch shift bussing tables at one restaurant and an evening shift bartending at another because his employers have leverage. They're well aware that his green card wasn't issued by USCIS but by some fulano on Twenty-Sixth Street, so his shifts are six hours each. He hits magic number thirty-six on his weekly paychecks, which means part-time. No benefits. No overtime. He gets pissed, but he's also happy to get hours.

Reaching the middle of beer four means it's going to turn into a long night. If we stop before "getting white-girl wasted," as he likes to say, it's at beer three. This is four, we haven't seen each other since I left for Iowa, and tomorrow is his only day off, so we won't stop until someone tells us we have to. The wet crack and sizzle of popping beer five brings that warm boozy blanket feeling, and things get loose. Octavio recounts how a woman walked in wearing the tightest dressy pantsuit he's ever seen.

"Cómo le dicen a esa madre?

"Cuál?"

"Eh. El dedo del camello!"

He's just a hair shorter than I am, maybe five foot five, but tonight he gets a couple of inches from his speckled wing-tips. He dresses the way my elementary school nuns said a man should: a crease down the legs of his pants, no sneakers, a shirt with a collar, and if it's cold out, a sweater, sometimes a turtleneck. He does this every day, despite the fact that after his morning or afternoon commute, he'll get to his first job and change into a uniform. He'll put his clothes back on for the five-minute drive to his second job, and change into a uniform again.

He's not exactly muscular, at least not like the symmetrical bros who pack into gyms to simulate work, carefully examining themselves in the mirror, and deliberately building aesthetic muscles, but when you slap his back it's hard, and so are his arms, especially the right one. I tried to count how many times he lifted bus pans full of everyone's dirty dishes one shift but lost count at around a hundred.

"Salud!"

"Órale."

He proposes a toast to Profesor Orduña, raising his can, spilling some beer on the floor. Cookie, who'd been wandering around our feet, rushes to lick it up. Octavio reaches out and tugs on my beard. He says he knew I would show up with a beard because I'm a professor now, and professors all around the world have beards. "It's true," I tell him. I've tried explaining that I'm a lowly teaching assistant, nothing like a professor, and that I have this beard because I'm too lazy to shave, and I can't afford razor cartridges, but he insists.

"Profesor Orduña, cabrón. No mames."

He revels in it, laughing, asking what the güeritos think when their teacher walks into the classroom and it's me. I tell him that sometimes I'm the first brown person these young people have ever seen in person, let alone spent meaningful time with, and that mostly, I think, the güeritos, güeritas, non-güeritos, and non-güeritas don't think, unless I expend inordinate amounts of energy forcing them to. Anyway, he gets a real kick out of it, and I guess I get a kick out of telling him.

Octavio tilts his head back, letting the last quarter can of Tecate rush down his throat, and then he jumps out of his chair with his index in the air.

"Tengo algo que enseñarte."

Last time he jumped out of his chair like this, brow tight, and the ends of his smile curling just a bit harder than usual, he retrieved a jarana made out of an armadillo carapace. This time it's a lime-green tin gasoline canister. He holds it out and motions with his head for me to take it.

"Ábrelo."

When I met Octavio he was in his early twenties. It was the first time I'd gone back to Mexico since my mom and I moved to Chicago when I was a baby. I remember the first long walk down the stone corridor that led to my grandmother's front door, the same corridor pictured in photos I'd seen of my mom holding me as an infant. Every couple of feet another teary-eyed stranger embraced me and told me how long they'd missed me.

"Hola, mijo. Soy tu tía Mica."

"Hola, mi amor."

"Hola, mijito."

One after another, faces I'd seen but couldn't remember kept coming, shaky-voiced and sobbing. It felt wrong I'd never heard of people so closely blood-related, or even worse, that if I had I'd completely forgotten them. I didn't know their names or the names of their children. I wasn't sure how many cousins I had. I didn't know the first thing about any of their lives.

At some point, an old woman with curly brown hair knelt before me, and I recognized her as my grandmother from a photograph. As she squeezed me, her warm tears soaked through my shirt and I remember feeling something I didn't understand at the time, the secondary emotion of shame at the nothingness I felt toward my grandmother, my father's mother, guilt, and a little anger at the strangeness of being held so tightly and missed so dearly by this weeping woman I knew nothing about, for whom I knew I *should* feel but couldn't.

This infant they'd once held came back to them as a nine-year-old, but the absence belonged only to them.

The languid, tropical evenings saturated in the hum of countless cicadas, the sun disappearing behind a white-tipped Citlaltépetl, this collection of faces were the things my father spent nights longing for while strumming his cracked guitar in our kitchen in Chicago. He'd been severed from what he was, and his once-mysterious future quickly became a trudging present of wage labor—the self-perpetuating cycle of hand to mouth. Even as a young child, I recognized a quality in his voice when he sang certain songs on some nights, the tones of a deep and abiding solitude. At the time, for me, the words he sang held no weight, but when I listen to them now, I remember my young father, younger than I am now, wailing about everything that had been taken from him.

At dusk, the evening of my homecoming, a band set up in the small courtyard next to a coffee tree and a wall of fuchsia bougainvillea. One of the musicians introduced himself as

Octavio and began playing a variation of "Noche Criolla," up-tempo for a bolero, and virtuosic—the Javier Solís version. The plinking of three men at a rosewood marimba and the chorus of voices behind Octavio made the song a celebration of a beautiful place and stripped it of the melancholy I liked and with which I had come to associate it because of my dad's version. Solís, who wasn't born in Veracruz, sings it with affect. You can sense the imitation of suffering in the smoothness of his voice, so it doesn't contain that quality of genuine woundedness some singers have when they sing certain songs. The version I'd always heard from our kitchen in Chicago was the version of Agustín Lara, the original composer, who sat alone at a piano, smoking unfiltered cigarettes while he sang it. Lara, who was born in Tlacotalpan, a sleepy town two hours from my grandmother's house, was sent to live at his aunt's hospice in Mexico City after his mother died. Unlike Solís, Lara's version ends on the image of staring into an expanse of darkness, and his voice comes to sound like a captured and wounded beast thrashing against its cage. That's how my dad sang his version, and that's how I liked it.

"Ábrelo, cabrón."

There's something swishing inside the canister, and I know it isn't gasoline. Mezcal, which is not a type of tequila, but is its own spirit, is neither my friend nor my enemy. It's more like someone who'll always be a friend despite the fact that he's stolen your significant other and wrecked your car. When I pop the top off, the smell of smoke and the shadow of a burning piña makes me nostalgic for the moments before blackout, when apprehension happens through a fine sieve: a pastiche of glittering lights, everything reduced to sensation, incredible levity, laughter, and the anticipation of that smooth darkness, the lost moments where the mind is jettisoned, at rest, quiet, and alone.

"Qué tal, guey?"

We're heading there tonight, and this mezcal will be our vehicle. Octavio retrieves two snifters from an armoire where he houses all of his best bottles. The mezcal, he says, is from Oaxaca, sent in the care of an old truck driver who carries things from southern Mexico to Reynosa, where his partner from the States picks them up and drives them to the Midwest.

"Como un FedEx mexicano."

"Pero FedEx existe en México, guey."

"No mames, cabrón. Como un FedEx *bien* mexicano."

He fills both snifters with the golden liquid, and in the dim room they catch the light and look like twin suns. He tells me to drink it slowly because it came a long way and deserves to be savored. He says it's what the güeros refer to as artisanal: that the guy who made it, made it from start to finish, one palenquero in his backyard. He explains that at one point there were hundreds of palenques in Oaxaca, little old men and women with backyard stills cultivating a diversity of maguey on their small patches of mountainside.

I take a sip of the liquid. It tastes like smoke and earth. It's similar in many ways to a Highland Scotch, intensely peaty, but sweeter, with a vague flavor of overripe fruit.

Octavio raises his glass and looks at it in the light. He says that the liquid that will take us a few seconds to drink took over a decade to make. He proposes a toast.

"Pa' las viejas."

I can tell he means our moms because he's getting more and more melancholic as the night goes on. Las viejas would be pissed if they saw us now. Mine would remind me that she hadn't worked so many hours in uniform rooms and restaurants, and that she and my father hadn't left home for me to drink swill until my throat is pink and raw in the very early morning. My voice mail is always full on weekend mornings, and it's always her, urging me to be careful, to eat well, not to drink so much. "And why don't you answer the phone, cabrón?" Even though she's often yelling, her voice sounds infinitely small and full of distress because she knows her son, knows what's usually going on when I don't answer for days. She's seen me at the end of a weeklong bender, and we both wonder how many more of those I can take. She says I'm melancholic like my father, but that seems like too calm a word, like a vessel with a small hole that sinks quietly into darkened water. More often than not, I feel on fire and am prone to destructive and self-destructive behavior. Sometimes, on the tail end of those benders, I manage to unmoor completely from reality.

Octavio Paz wrote in *The Labyrinth of Solitude*, "Man is the only being who knows he is alone," and he asserted that "nostalgia and a search for communion" is what we are. I'm not so sure. I've seen apes at the zoo that seem to know better than most of my students and peers that they are utterly alone in the universe, and I've known many people who are giddy in and oblivious to their ultimate solitude. I'm also not convinced that the nostalgia everyone says is a looking backward isn't a look into an alternate future, one that's always better than the miserable present, a necessary and necessarily unreachable place to make the soul more able to withstand the brutality of the real. The Octavio sitting across from me pours another mezcal and says he misses his mom. For him, the knowledge of his solitude is not the result of bookish ennui. It is not an ontological consideration. This is his life, the condition and sensations of exile in which he finds himself. His solitude is not an abstraction, and it renews itself every day. There's a happy narrative, a myth created by others about immigrants, and even by some immigrants themselves about "the Immigrant experience." It's a story of upward mobility that starts once we cross the border, and it never properly addresses the ways prosperity in the United States is intimately tied to misery elsewhere. I've known several people to go back, to leave this supposed dream because it becomes miserable for them. It's difficult to establish happiness and a necessary sense of communion with members of a society that allow for you, in actuality and in representation, the space of a maid, a nanny, a janitor, a day laborer, or a landscaper, and nothing else.

Still, Octavio manages to do exactly this, be happy, not all the time, and certainly not with the graces of the United States, but in spite of them. On the Internet, he has as many friends from home as he does from this place, and although his English isn't the best, he writes to people in it, and they seem to manage some understanding. He congratulates friends when they post wedding pictures and snapshots of their newborns wrapped in hospital sheets, he expresses discontent in the comment sections of news articles, and he links to popular songs he's into. Every day, he encounters US-born individuals, some of whom probably know he's undocumented, and, at least in their daily interactions, they don't seem to care, or they don't want to know, and they leave him alone, greet him warmly, and leave him tips. He says there's a regular at the bar where he works, an old Korean War vet who tells him a dirty joke in English every time he's there. More often than not people leave him alone, and he's gotten used to the rhythm of life here. Sometimes he says he even feels comfortable until something reminds him that his reality has very sharp edges.

In writing about threat in our contemporary American milieu, Canadian philosopher and social theorist Brian Massumi says, "We live in times when what has not happened qualifies as front-page news." The specific *what-has-not-happened* that exists in the media and in the minds of an increasing number of people around the globe is distilled in a poster I've seen in which a US soldier advances while pointing his M16. Behind him is a map of the United States, a waving US flag, a man wearing a turban holding an AK-47, and brown bodies hopping a wrought-iron fence. The tagline: "One war, two fronts."

Octavio and I have been made representations of what Massumi calls the "self-renewing menace potential." We are the "future reality of threat," the threat that America will not remain American, and what this really means is the possibility that the United States will not remain white and English-language-dominated. And who is scared of that?

Octavio and I might also be reminders of the permeability of all boundaries, of the limits of law enforcement, of a waning power, of the inherent violence that guarantees the idea of citizenship. Liberal democratic states are supposed to hold true that all people, by virtue of being human, have certain universal rights, and that these things called rights do not need to be earned, because we always already have them. Simultaneously we're also always subject to a number of bodies of law, depending on the governing structures in which we live. But people like Octavio and to a lesser extent me—people who live within the territory of one state but aren't citizens of that state—are somehow moved into a zone in which the universality of rights does not reach us. Rather than meaning we are ignored or unbound by law, we exist with disproportionate amounts of law construed only as restriction, exclusion, deprivation, and punishment.

Octavio is the exclusion, and even though he's here, he isn't. There is an entire body of law to ensure he is never fully here.

When I check my flip phone for the time, I have to close one eye to read the digital numbers. It's three seventeen in the morning, and the canister of mezcal has gotten us both very drunk.

"O, O, O, cabrón! Se me olvidó decirte."

Octavio slurs his words a bit, and his eyes have that too-relaxed slant. He tells me he was driving home after picking up his wife from work when he was pulled over for making a U-turn.

"Y me dejó ir."

"Te dejó ir? Así nada más?"

I don't know if he fully appreciates how many people have been deported after minor traffic violations, how close he came to another starting over after he'd just started getting over the previous one, or how he narrowly escaped being permanently barred from the United States. If it had been a different police officer, or maybe the same one in a different mood a minute or two before or after, it might have been the boot. But when the cop asked why he'd pulled a U-turn, he told him in all earnestness that he had an emergency. When the cop asked him what the emergency was, he told him it was his wife, that she was hungry. He said the cop chuckled a little and then scolded him, saying that wasn't an emergency, to which he'd replied, "Sir, you should see my wife." Then the cop lost it and let him off with a warning.

In *Discipline and Punish*, Michel Foucault poses Jeremy Bentham's model prison as the emergent paradigm of state power:

> Hence the major effect of the Panopticon: to induce in the inmate a state of conscious and permanent visibility that assures the automatic functioning of power. So to arrange things that the surveillance is permanent in its effects, even if it is discontinuous in its action; that the perfection of power should tend to render its actual exercise unnecessary.

Octavio raises his snifter. The last bit of mezcal swirls up the side and almost catches air.

"Let's go for a drink!" he yells.

For better or worse, he has yet to become "the principle of his own subjection," and sometimes he seems to fully let go of giving a fuck. He lived through a banking crisis, the peso crisis, urbanization, and so-called structural adjustment. Now he's here. When he was a kid he and his family lived on a plot of land they owned without a deed, something that used to be common. But each season, the same amount of work made them less able to live, until they had to abandon their plot and move to an unincorporated area outside the closest city. He lived in a cinderblock and concrete structure he and his brother built until things became unlivable there too. He says he couldn't just stay there and wait to die, so he decided to go north like many of the other men had. He knew a group of brothers who were planning to go to New York. He asked if he could join their group. They said yes.

CHAPTER 5

A Civilized Man

It's my second time here in Des Moines, and it's discon-
certing that the Neal Smith Federal Building is becoming
familiar. Time and again I catch myself staring into the black
granite walls where my reflection becomes a vague outline—
no expression, no features, only a hollow black figure that
shares my shape and follows me through the silence and ste-
rility of these empty halls.

"How can I help you?"

My appointment is several floors up this time. A terse
young woman greets me as I push through two glass doors
that open into a small reception area. Posted behind her is an
armed guard who silently shifts his weight from foot to foot,
his hands fixed on his hips, fingertips floating centimeters
from his handcuffs and gun. The office is reminiscent of a
first-class airline lounge, where the layout is designed to keep
those on the outside from even seeing inside.

She points to a clipboard on the counter and asks for
proof that I'm allowed to be there. The guard looks like he's
in his mid-fifties but has round, boyish features, and he's
staring at me with his hands on his belt. I open my shoulder bag with slow, deliberate movements. His deep green
uniform in such close proximity references former abuses,
like the "random" nature of frequent stops and the feeling of

wide, forceful hands digging through your pockets. It signi-
fies the volatile rhythm of Maglites tapping in the palms of
uniformed men, the threat that at any moment you could
be placed in the back of a cop car, like you'd seen done to
your friend, driven to a place where no one would see or no
one would care to see, only to be released a few hours later,
bruised and bleeding, with a verbal warning. His uniform
dredges the face of a fourteen-year-old as he's pulled away
in a backseat cage, his eyes holding an absolute zero only
achievable after living through something like war.

My upper lip starts to sweat under my moustache. I can
feel my entire body become damp, and I sense every droplet of perspiration that gathers enough mass to drip down
my spine. Minuscule movements become foreign, almost as
though they're on slight delay, as if it isn't me making them.
We both know everything in my possession has already been
X-rayed, and I've just been made to walk through a metal
detector downstairs. He knows a security wand has been run
over the surface of my body, but he gazes blackly for too long
anyway. I telegraph everything I do.

His face is like an impermeable wall atop his green uniform. I can't detect any hint of expression. I try but can't tell
if he's making calculations or if he's staring elsewhere—no-
where—lobotomized by long stretches of idle time. I wonder
if he daydreams scenarios, like I do, in which he becomes a
hero, and if his involve discharging his weapon since he carries one.

The black metal butt of his handgun peaks from the
holster, and I recall an occasion when a friend yelled at me
for picking up his rifle, saying that his weapon was an instrument of death, that when he picked it up he became a
killer, whether he killed something or not because everyone
who possesses a firearm has on some level made the deci-
sion they are willing to kill. I read somewhere that homicidal
ideation is incredibly common among the general population, but even before I knew this I was never alarmed when

visions that ended in me killing someone would materialize rather comprehensively in my mind. These scenarios usually crept up near the edge of train platforms and were tinged with something of an uncanny sensation because they felt as though they were coming from somewhere beyond my will, making the acts seems inevitable and, in a strange way, already done. On the rare occasion I'm in very close proximity to someone wearing a gun, I imagine grabbing it. I keep my hands at my side.

Judging others' apprehension is never easy. He might be looking past me, past everything. His blond eyebrows are flat, his mouth flat. His eyes are unmoving pools of pale blue. It wouldn't matter if he were someone different, someone indifferent, because in his uniform he's the operator of an institutional function. He may not know it, but he's guarding a kind of property called citizenship. His flat demeanor somehow feels aggressive to me. His unmoving eyes aren't looking at me, but I can feel them gazing nonetheless. His stillness is unreadable.

The thoughts, predilections, and motivations of the person inside the guard are in many ways irrelevant. I think some jobs are ones a moral person can't do, and this may be one of them, even though he's just sitting here. Gazing at his hip, at the one metal clasp that catches the neon office light and keeps his gun in place, I understand him to be an embodied reference to state violence, the same way gang colors signal not only allegiance but former violence committed by one's gang.

Maybe this is where the real power is most evident, in this stillness, in this inaction that nevertheless enforces the boundaries of the state. The power is doubled in my recognition of the authority he signals, in *my* internalization of the power he represents, *my* feeling that his eyes are upon me, *my* sitting here thinking about him sitting there. So I approach the desk slowly, move my hands slowly, sliding my summons from between the pages of a notebook, and carefully placing the single sheet of paper on the counter.

Inside the large, nearly empty waiting room a couple—a young kid who looks Mexican and a young white woman with big hoop earrings and meticulously gelled baby hair on her forehead—lean toward their lawyer, a young white man in an ill-fitting suit the color of fog. The gray washes him out, blends into his pale complexion, making him look like an overexposed photograph, one in which you can't see anyone's facial features but still know who they are. The lawyer leans forward awkwardly, like he's attempting to crease his suit's fabric as little as possible or like he hasn't become comfortable wearing it yet. He whispers something to his young clients, which I can't hear. The three of them sit facing me a few rows away, so I try to read the counsel's lips. It's useless—he's a fast talker and his mouth barely moves. Mostly silent, the clients periodically exchange bewildered looks. One peculiar word does seem to be repeated. Each time it's spoken it causes the couple to sink closer toward each other. The word seems to start with a hard "C," followed immediately by an "R" that shapes the counsel's mouth into a tense pucker, then two rapid flashes of his slightly yellowed teeth. After the last repetition, his young, brown-skinned client, who had already been looking toward the floor, runs his hands hard on the back of his buzz cut. Because I'm here for my civics interview, and because the couple is here with their lawyer, it dawns on me that they might be here for a Stokes interview, the interview that comes after a couple applying for immigration relief based on marriage fails to convince an official during their first interview that their relationship is "genuine." Next to him, his wife, who sometimes looks nineteen and other times about twelve, delicately brings her hand just above his shoulder blades. She hesitates before placing it on his back, and in that moment the kid sinks into himself. She moves it gently in small circles.

Counsel repeats the word, which I finally make out: *Christmas.*

Christmas, I mouth, wondering why this lawyer would discuss Christmas on a summer day with his clients, and why it seemed so unsettling to them. Outside, the harsh midday sun amplifies itself on the mirrored exterior of the adjacent high-rise. It cuts through a large window behind them that frames their bodies. For a moment they're still, and they look like posed figures in a Renaissance painting. I find myself scanning them for objects of significance. A tiny spectrum glints from a set stone on the ring finger of the young woman's left hand. The baby-faced attorney clutches a black leather folio, as if for balance. A US flag hangs limp in the corner without the possibility of flight in the windless room. The reflection of an armed guard hovers ghostlike and watching. Sunk in the middle is the figure of a sullen man—a dark, heavy spot that affects everything around it—his brown skin making him the primary object of this scene.

It looks so composed, for a moment I think about taking their photo, but instead I just sketch their long slender extremities on the back of a government booklet I'd been given to study. More than their semblance, I'm interested in what's not going on around them, in the invisible relations that hold everything here in place, the still tension with which they sit and hang on their lawyer's every word. This building houses the administrative arm of the immigration apparatus, the place where the single sheets of paper that can change everything about a person's life are printed, signed, stamped, or examined and passed along. This is the castle of papers, the papers I'd grown up hearing so much about. But how does one apprehend, let alone capture, these muted bonds, these minute movements, these paperwork and keystroke power structures that build and sustain American empire?

The young brown man's presence in this office, and the fact that his new bride and attorney flank him, means they've probably already failed a little. It means that during their first interview they didn't convince the interviewer theirs was a bona fide marriage, whatever that means. The young man who I believe is undocumented is now in a more precarious place than before he started because there is no turning back. Before, he was in the relative safety of contingent anonymity. The state didn't know who he was, where he lived, or what his name was, but now he's provided all that previously guarded information on forms he filled out himself. He has completely exposed himself, and so far it does not seem good.

The attorney closes his eyes and nods gently. To feign concern is not part of his job—it's a personal courtesy, an added bonus, or maybe he does care. Maybe his outward display is genuine, in which case, as an immigration attorney he'll have to learn not to care so much, to do his best, yes, but not lose sleep over every deported individual, because there have been many, and there will continue to be many. Doctors know this: they have to steel themselves, go significantly cold in order to continue working dispassionately amid a relentless succession of sorrows. The attorney's role is to know the complicated matrix of always-shifting immigration law—an intractable knot of specialized language—and guide them through as best he can. If the couple had to go to immigration court and could not afford his representation, they would not be granted legal counsel by the state. Their separation would be much more likely. He knows this. With the rest of his knowledge, which he exchanges for money, he'll grant them access to the law.

The waiting room is silent except for the faint whir of a large plasma screen mounted on the wall. Reclined in an ergonomic office chair, the armed guard watches a middle-aged man sell his grandfather's World War II uniform on a muted episode of *Pawn Stars*. He stares blankly at the high-definition imagery that flashes on the monitor. I avert my eyes because the rapid succession of hyper-saturated HD color irritates my eyes.

I scrawl "Adoration in Waiting" underneath my terrible

drawing because the young couple and their lawyer bring to mind those figures transfixed in religious adoration from High Renaissance art. I'd seen such an image a few months earlier that had broken something of itself off, lodged slivers of its furtive psychology, in my mind. I'd been walking through the J. Paul Getty Museum in a sort of torpor brought on by the excesses of the sprawling grounds: the precisely manicured topiary, the reverberation of my footsteps through the hollow corridors, the ornate galleries full of private riches. It wasn't immediately clear why the painting made such an impression, but after leaving it and winding through room upon room of opulent relics, I'd ended up back in front of it. Surrounded by luxury and light, the austerity of the painting provided a hole to sink into. I found myself sepulchered in Caspar's sinister gaze.

I wanted to take a photograph of the painting and its corresponding placard, so I casually turned in both directions looking for the guards who had been posted at the doorway, but they were gone. The plaque read "Adoration of the Magi." The artist: Venetian painter Andrea Mantegna. The reliquary had emptied—I was alone—so I snapped three pictures, the last of which was a close-up of Caspar's pale face. His head was slightly tilted downward, mouth ajar, and eyes fixed on a far-off point. He looked like a caged animal that hadn't been fed for days, a fresh kill dangling somewhere in the distance. His look was lecherous and had such a draw that several weeks passed before I noticed the blessing bestowed by the Christ child while looking over my photographs of that day.

Looking at it for the second time made me feel claustrophobic. I was dropped into Caspar's perversion once again—his lust-filled eyes, his slightly open mouth. I was repulsed but nonetheless transfixed. It seemed illicit, blasphemous, that his agency commanded more of the frame than the Christ child's. Initially I'd been drawn to it because its characters weren't surrounded by opulence, like the other paintings lining the walls, but instead buried in total darkness. Less a celebration of divinity born, it was a dark allegory luring me toward the fissures in the characters' inner lives.

In the waiting room in Des Moines the scene is more ambiguous, but I can't shake the feeling they're somehow related. Looking at the Department of Homeland Security seal evokes a familiar repulsion, one that wells up inside me when I'm in the vicinity of this kind of power. In the museum, Caspar seemed drunk at the potential outcome of his transaction: a precious Chinese cup to secure His grace, his conspicuous adoration—he a kneeling sovereign—in exchange for the keys to a higher kingdom. Mantegna was born on the cusp of an emerging order. In his time, Cosimo de' Medici would have established his bank as the official lending institution of the Catholic Church, skirting the divine ban on usury with an unprecedented system of leveraged finance. Shortly thereafter, the Medici bank would guarantee a lavish papal overdraft for which they would be granted the right to collect tithes.

Before the age of thirty, Mantegna would rise to prominence as court painter for the powerful Gonzaga family of Mantua, where he would live through the ascension of northern Italian cities as independent, international centers of commodity-based finance. He would witness the genuflection of feudal lords before bankers, the excommunication of clergy for not paying their debts, and the divine right of kings dissolve before a new logic. He and his patron, Ludovico II Gonzaga, a mercenary general, were at the vanguard of an emergent economic order that would dissolve the absolute power of kings and give way to new structures of power based on trade, finance, and capital in an economy and mode of governance growing to a new scale.

In the waiting room there are no kings, only the Department of Homeland Security. The body of the sovereign, an easily identifiable locus of power, is absent, but the images are intrinsically linked in my mind. The old image by Mantegna, produced around 1500, reflects an empire teetering on the verge of modernity—a Europe hungry to supplant the transcendence of God with more earthly transactions. The scene in this room seems to exist on a continuum with that emergence. The four of us in this room wait seated before a disembodied authority, an authority allegedly diffused to all of us, handled through administrators and managers. The brown man might be the object of adoration in this waiting room because the state requires bodies to support it. In this North American context, Mexicans have served this purpose well. We've been used as disposable, malleable bodies that can be drawn in and purged according to labor demands and cyclical xenophobic trends.

If it is as I suspect, and the young couple's summons is for a marriage fraud interview, then they will be questioned by trained interrogators.

"What did you get your wife last Christmas?"

This might have been what their attorney was mouthing, possibly attempting to coach them through a scenario he thought was possible in the interview rooms. As their attorney, he must have already informed them that the process would end with the state granting or not granting their love written legitimacy, and that failure was a very real possibility.

"It would mean deportation," he probably said in solemn tones, twiddling a pen nervously between his fingertips.

"It would mean being permanently barred from the country. You would never be able to adjust."

He clarifies for good measure: "Never be able to come back."

Acute ticks would have suddenly become audible, maybe from an old clock on the wall. Somewhere in his subconscious, the attorney would imagine what it would be like to be under that kind of pressure. The young white lady would feel her face flush, feel her cheeks suddenly rush with heat. A line of perspiration would emerge and then begin to run down the channel of the attorney's back. His pale face would have turned bright red as he informed them that the state might ask questions about their partner's intimate clothing: what color, what cut, what size.

"Does your wife prefer boy shorts or thongs?"

"What kind of birth control do you use?"

If he's a thorough lawyer, he will let them know that if they're lucky, they'll get an investigator who's mostly disinterested and cold.

"Don't be surprised if they cut you off. That's good, just move on."

He would explain the opposite scenario, the possibility of getting someone who believes himself or herself to be a gatekeeper, thinks he or she is doing good work, wakes up in the morning eager to make sure "America is secure." Counsel's knuckles will turn white as he squeezes his pen, looks at his male client, and explains that in this situation the investigator will be crass, perhaps even vulgar—that he'll look smug at delicate moments, trying to provoke in him an emotional and volatile state.

"Tell me, does your wife have any distinguishing marks in places usually covered by clothes?"

Counsel will tell them they'll have to answer these kinds of questions.

"Remain calm. No matter what."

The girl will look at her young husband, run her hand down the back of his head, fingering a fibrous line of scar tissue. She'll imagine his body suddenly jutting across a table, a hand grabbing at the investigator's face.

"Calm. No matter what."

Inside the interview room, small bureaucrats are made insurmountable. It takes a minuscule reason, or no reason at all, to raise suspicions about the authenticity of a marriage. The criteria the US Citizenship and Immigration Services use to determine whether a marriage is bona fide or not is vague and based on institutionally held normative models of marriage. I know at least one couple who would surely fail even though they've been married for over twenty years, because they've never lived in the same state, shared a bank account, or spent more than a couple of days a year together. And until very recently, when the federal government started recognizing same-sex unions, only heterosexual couples could be granted immigration relief through marriage. A few scribbled notes on a sheet of paper, a few boxes checked or unchecked, and the couple can formally be called a fraud, with little recourse to appeal. A few keystrokes and the young brown man will officially be categorized "removable," and deportation proceedings might automatically be triggered.

The only people allowed in this second-floor waiting room are those on either end of this official USCIS business, so the particularities of this kind of administrative population control aren't widely seen. As I sit staring at the three of them, I wonder how many marriages between people I know would pass this test. I know my own parents probably stayed married during various rough periods in their relationship because they couldn't afford to get divorced or because they knew they wouldn't be able to sustain themselves financially without the other's income. How can an arrangement based on tangible, sometimes material needs be deemed fraudulent when that is exactly the basis of so many marriages, many of them happy and enduring?

The young man looks up, and at first I think he catches me staring at his wife, but he hasn't. He shoots me a reverse nod: one sudden upward jerk of the chin. It's a question that varies slightly with the forcefulness of the jerk. I know it means "qué pedo?" It could mean "qué pedo, cabrón?" but it doesn't. I shoot it back with an equal force, and now they both mean hello—now it's the recognition of sharing something in common, because we both know that we know a substantial thing about the other simply by being in this room together. We stare at each other for a moment before we both turn away. It had been comfortable to place myself in the role of a spectator watching from a safe and comfortable distance, but I too was in this room, waiting to be evaluated and waiting to underwrite the legitimacy of the dehumanizing categories in which I have lived.

We are, of course, not in the same predicament. My presence here is more or less a formality, provided I'm not caught committing any felonies, certain misdemeanors, or any crimes of moral turpitude prior to the oath ceremony. I look down at the booklet in my right hand, the one I'd been given to study. On the cover Mount Rushmore dissolves into an undulating US flag. George Washington's stone face looks out beyond the horizon. I think about Mantegna, how his own desires may have been reflected in Caspar's expression, the slacked jaw, the downward tilt of his head, the lust in his eyes. Caspar looks upon the Christ child, understanding that his kingdom is for sale. When Mantegna made his painting, he and others like him had ascended to the kind of life previously reserved for royalty or clergy, but rather than signaling the dismantling of structures of power, as such, power simply adapted to a new world. It feels like we are living in a similar moment.

A young woman in a dressy pantsuit comes through a door that leads to a hallway beyond the waiting room. It's a hallway lined with cubicles in which the banal task of sorting populations is done through the orderly processing of forms, the evaluation of answers to standardized questions, and spreadsheet analysis. She calls the man's name. She smiles genuinely at him and holds the door as they enter.

CHAPTER 6

Good Moral Character

From outside the window, construction cranes cast long shadows on the hotel curtains. I put my bags down and go to the balcony, which overlooks a group of workers smoking cigarettes in the depressed concrete foundation. A few pieces of bare rebar jut out of the flat gray surface and extend upward, looking like the cleanly picked bones in an upturned carcass. The cranes slowly track over development in Metro Manila. The blood-orange sky makes the reflective skyscrapers look as if they're hemorrhaging.

At my last appointment the US government determined I was "of good moral character" by evaluating my responses to a series of inane questions. Had I ever been a habitual drunkard? Been a prostitute or with a prostitute? Had I ever sold or smuggled controlled substances, illegal drugs, narcotics? Had I ever been married to more than one person at the same time? Had I ever helped anyone enter or try to enter the United States illegally? What about gambling? Had I ever received income from illegal gambling? Had I failed to support any dependents or failed to pay alimony? Had I ever committed a crime for which I was never arrested? The fact that my record was clean meant that in their eyes I was one of the good ones, and I had done something or not done something to receive the benefit of no longer being subject to a punitive body of law that is arguably the most, or one of the most, complicated in the United States. The woman who asked me this series of questions seemed rather uninterested in my answers, but still, as she rattled them off, I wondered what my fate would have been if my answers had been different, if they had pulled images and information from social media to determine my moral character, or if they'd simply talked with friends, acquaintances, ex-friends, and ex-acquaintances. I wondered too how many of the affluent kids I went to high school with—sons and daughters of politicians, news anchors, and high-ranking business officials— would pass this kind of test.

Having lived as a permanent resident through my teens and early twenties had been an incredibly reckless thing to do. In retrospect I'm not sure what my parents were thinking in not putting me through this process as soon as I qualified. In 1996 the Illegal Immigration Reform and Immigrant Responsibility Act expanded the list of deportable offenses by several orders of magnitude, and things many of the kids I went to high school with were doing on a daily basis, sometimes several times a day, were deportable offenses. I could have been forcibly removed from the country, severing all associations with the people, places, and things that had become home. Minor crimes friends and peers were able to expunge from their records, things cops gave them warnings for, or things they weren't even stopped for because of who they were and how they looked could have gotten me deported. I can't imagine my reality if that had come to pass, and I can't believe I'd walked that line for so long. The amount of luck involved in never having been caught doing things that teenagers do seemed supernatural, but maybe it had to do with who I hung around with, in what spaces, and the protection those associations offered. I'd had several close calls with law enforcement, sometimes having been stopped because of the way I look, but they somehow all ended favorably for me, because, I think, I'd immediately played the game of demonstrating that I was, in fact, "one of the good ones" by choosing a "higher" register in which to speak and mentioning where I went to school.

As I waited for the next certified letter telling me where and when my naturalization ceremony would take place, an opportunity to travel to the Philippines presented itself. I would be able to go, free of charge, as a fellow for a graduate writing workshop that would take place on various islands throughout the country.

I'd been one of the last fellows to book my flight, so the rest of the writers' group was staying at another hotel. I read that it wasn't a great idea to leave the country during the naturalization process and if it could be avoided, it should. The trip was especially troubling considering the amount of time I'd be gone, the potential to miss the actual ceremony, and the potential to get into some kind of trouble that would prevent me from completing the very last step in becoming a citizen of the United States. If I missed the ceremony it could technically be rescheduled, but a failure to respond promptly to the government's certified letters while missing appointments could end in the denial of the application in this final stage. Despite all this, a free trip to Southeast Asia was too good to pass up.

My room at the A. Venue in Makati City is small but luxurious, and it has a Western toilet. It's reminiscent of one of those boutique hotels in the Meatpacking District in Manhattan—the ones that staff their bellhop positions with tall men who look like male models—except here we'd been warned not to drink the water, to use bottled to brush our teeth, and to be discerning about the establishments in which we took ice in our beverages. "They'll like you," I'd been told, "because you look like one of their celebrities."

Below the window, the group of laborers has finished their cigarettes, resumed their work. On an adjacent street, a man and woman push a makeshift cart toward an empty lot, and as I turn away from the window, movement in the bed of the cart catches my eye. Looking back, I see a small boy in a bright yellow tank top the color of cartoon birds. He could be two years old or perhaps a malnourished three or four. A small girl, about the same size, sits on what looks like a pile of rags in the cart. Nestled in her lap, an infant gropes at her long black hair. Then the cart and its contents disappear below a sheet of corrugated tin that tops a small structure they've made between construction sites.

Jeremiah, a nonpracticing Jew from Alabama, whom I've known for a couple of years, will be my roommate for the trip. He's a lanky man who always seems to be in a state of bewilderment, as though he were moving through the world seeing everything for the first time. We took separate flights, and, characteristically for both of us, we failed to coordinate our arrivals in any way. Before I can start worrying, though, I see Jeremiah across the hotel lobby examining the texture of one of the walls.

"Oh, hey," he says, smiling when he sees me walking toward him.

Makati City is the financial center of the Philippines. After dark, everything bleached by the sun glows in disquietude under the blinking of neon signs. S-Class Mercedes pull out of embassies and multinational headquarters into teeming streets, where they roll so slowly Jeremiah and I can observe the individual revolutions of each wheel. A skinny old woman with a white braid dangling down to the small of her back pushes past us, somehow able to move a rolling food stand three times her size. She takes care not to get too close to the luxury vehicles, instead opting to almost roll over the foot of a child sitting on the curb. English-language Revlon advertisements featuring a smiling Halle Berry hang on the street lamps, while emaciated dogs tear at husks and overripe fruit caked in the gutter.

Less than a block from the hotel, we find ourselves walking down a dark street lined with bars that advertise women. Inside my right pocket, I feel the jagged edge of a cracked Ambien left over from the transcontinental flight. For a second I consider not taking it, but I know our drinks will be watered down and overpriced, so I gather saliva and swallow the pill. We turn onto Makati Avenue, a long strip of twenty-four-hour fast-food restaurants and twenty-four-hour bank branches. The glass fronts of ChinaBank and 7-Eleven throb in the magenta light of an adjacent girly bar, and inside large guards in navy blue uniforms and aviators keep watch with arm-length assault rifles and pistol-grip shotguns. I begin to wonder what the consequences of having several loose pills on my person would be if caught, but I don't worry too much because the authorities don't seem concerned with anything but registers and moneyboxes. Outside, the avenue is clogged with middle-aged white men looking over groups of twelve- and thirteen-year-old girls as if picking produce at the market. A white man I later hear speaking Dutch, with a belly that hangs over his elastic waistband so far he can't see down to his curled yellow toenails, walks with each arm slung around a young Filipina, clearly underage, barely clothed. A young man with shiny spiked hair and a pinstriped black button-down shirt open to mid-chest is led by the hand by a heavily made-up girl who looks like she could be in middle school. This is the so-called Third World, seen as a sordid Disneyland, a repository for the West's most uninhibited fantasies. The red-light industry is the fourth-largest sector in the Philippine gross national product, and the averted gaze is part of protecting commercial interests too.

Jeremiah and I settle on a New Orleans–themed bar just off the main drag. I was drawn to the rakish dive by my own perverted desire to observe the remnant wounds of colonial powers fighting for landmass and constituent bodies, the subsequent colonization, and the forty-year "tutelage" in democracy. It's too dark to be sure, and the Ambien has started to take effect, but it seems like there's a full-sized American muscle car attached to the ceiling toward the end of the bar. Once Americans had been surprised not to be greeted as liberators in the Philippines. Now the ones who are still around are glad to be tourists and customers. A sinewy waste—gray hair and a Harley Davidson tee with the sleeves cut off— paws a Filipina who is sitting next to him trying not to look disgusted. He seems glad to have found a place where he can be the truest version of himself, and I'm glad too, to be on this side of the global order, allowed to wallow in the spoils of democracy even though my passport is not yet blue.

Before we order our whiskeys, several sets of hands slide up and under our shirts. "Would you like massage, ma'amsir?" "Buy me a drink, ma'amsir." Each of us is the center of a huddle of taut brown bodies wrapped in plastic made to look like leather, women from the countryside or several generations removed, victims of having been born into the continuity of imperialism from which there is little way out. The Ambien has a numbing effect on my body so that all the hands running across my skin feel like one rhythmic throbbing. Jeremiah has drawn more women, perhaps because in the dark his skin glows lighter. He proposes a toast to my impending "transition," which the women react to with confused expressions. One of them grabs hold of my crotch.

"Not that," I say, trying to squirm my way out of her grip.

He tells them about my upcoming naturalization ceremony, and they all seem to understand what this means. One of them points to a cake at the end of the bar and says they were about to celebrate her birthday and we can share. Most of them seem drunk or high already, a few of them are unsteady on their long, thin heels. "Cheers." *Clink.* Everyone does a shot for the birthday woman. A couple of the drunker ones grab chunks of cake off their plates and try to shove some into our mouths.

The bar is nearly empty except for the women who work there, so the crowd around us keeps swelling. They're at work, so each one struggles past the others to rub various parts of their shiny bodies against ours. The so-called expat in the Harley shirt, really just an émigré like the rest of us, grows his own crowd around him. He raises a glass to us, which we awkwardly and reflexively turn away from, thinking we are somehow distinct from him (and wanting to be). The women understand better, though. They understand the commodity character their breasts and genitals bear, and that we are already in various kinds of transactions. They'd seen us walk through the door, and we weren't yet gone. Places like these are stages for what Alphonso Lingis, American philosopher, writer, and translator, refers to as the "theater of libido," and we'd come for the performance of which the audience is always a part.

Throughout the Philippines there are populations of "Amerasians," the name given to the unclaimed children of servicemen conceived during the almost century-long US military presence. They represent the intersections of various kinds of subjugation that are transcultural and transhistoric. The fathers are always the Americans, never the mothers. If their father is white and the child resembles him, the child might receive some benefit from an aquiline nose and lighter skin. If the child's father is black, the child will be ostracized in proportion to his or her blackness. The Department of Homeland Security recognizes and provides preferential immigration status to Amerasians from Cambodia, Korea, Laos, Thailand, or Vietnam born after December 31, 1950, and before October 22, 1982. Filipino Amerasians are excluded. The largest concentration of these paternally unclaimed Filipino offspring is in Angeles City, the center of the Philippine sex industry, and home of Clark Air Base, a former US Air Force stronghold. The reasoning for the exclusion of Filipino Amerasians from immigration relief is that they were conceived and born during a period of occupation, which is technically considered peacetime, and that they are widely believed to have been conceived from prostitution. Recognizing them would mean tacitly recognizing that US forces participated in the sex trade for a prolonged period of time and en masse.

I'd crossed a threshold at the door of the bar with crisp bills from the ATM across the street. I'd nodded hello and thank you to the guard and his shotgun as he ensured the safety of my cash withdrawal. After the second shot of whiskey, a string of tiny blue Christmas lights bloom like hydrangeas from behind the bar. My libido has brought me here as a representative, and inside the dimly lit space I understand my desire is closer to compulsion than I had known. *L'objet petit a*—the unattainable object of desire—represented by the rising and waning rhythms of writhing bodies. A thick, very young woman approaches, and my gaze becomes fixed on the crease that runs from her inner thigh to her hip as she walks. She sits on my lap and squeezes my hardened dick. A very good man wouldn't have walked into this bar, and a good one would have left after this.

A few days later, the group of writers travels to Dumaguete in the province of Negros Oriental, the southeastern half of the island of Negros. One of the first things Jeremiah and I notice in our new location is a laminated list of rules posted near the elevator of our hostel. The bulleted commands seem mainly to be aimed at curtailing cohabitation with someone of the opposite gender. We share a look, and without saying it, I think we both get the impression that this is a religious establishment. Near the list there's a locked plastic bin with items for sale, and included among the shampoo and snack items are rosaries and small pocket Bibles. We don't give it much thought until we decide to cross the street and go for a walk on the stone esplanade along the waterfront. As we approach we see a sculpture of a canoe full of nuns, raised on a spout of water, all wearing black habits topped with large white cornettes that look like rams' horns. Jeremiah points to a plaque that explains these were French missionaries who arrived on these shores in 1904 looking to save souls less than a decade after the United States paid Spain twenty million dollars to annex the entire Philippine archipelago in the Treaty of Paris. The Philippine Revolution against the United States officially started in 1899 and officially ended in 1902. On Negros and elsewhere, indigenous rebel groups collectively referred to as the Irreconcilables continued fighting in opposition to the sale of their country, which they viewed as an illegitimate transfer of power because the Philippines was not, and had never been, for Spain to sell or for the United States to purchase.

Jeremiah and I continue along the boardwalk. The air is saturated in humidity, and I can feel sweat dripping. I squint, and for a moment this looks like it could be Veracruz— brown-skinned people walking on the Spanish-built structure, vendors selling flowers and small trinkets, and palm trees dropping their green oval seeds everywhere. We amble for a few minutes before bumping into another pair of writers, and we decide to spend the afternoon drinking beer at a small restaurant that overlooks the water.

As the sun approaches the horizon, shadows crawl across the street and into the water as though they're going home. We hear a distant racket like a rowdy party, faint but heading in our direction. One of the writers we're with says we should be heading back because our group is being greeted with dinner and a reading by scholars from the Silliman University National Writers Workshop, but several of us decide to stay. Over the next few minutes the sound grows until we see in the distance a bright, multicolored mass coming toward us down the middle of the street.

Early evening in Dumaguete is a warm blue that signals evening but is somehow still bright. There are floats elaborately adorned with local flowers and shiny metallic ribbons, and crowds have gathered on both sides of the road. We decide to get a closer look, so we settle our bill and push our way toward the street. When we finally make it through, we emerge onto a row of brawny men standing side by side, their hands folded in front of their chests in Catholic prayer. They wear giant silver angel wings and white satin robes with gold trim. Street lamps highlight their wings in orange, and they tremble in the faint breeze.

A young man selling flowers made out of tissue paper approaches us with his white bucket. He's tall and dark, with a broad nose and wide shoulders. He's painted a small crowned figure onto his plastic bucket, a figure that looks to be draped in some kind of robe. When the French nuns arrived on the shores of Negros, several groups of indigenous peasants who had been fighting the Spanish were then fighting both the Americans and European missionaries. These indigenous and peasant groups had been engaged in various forms of resistance since Ferdinand Magellan claimed the Philippine archipelago for Spain in 1521. By the time the French nuns hit Negros, the peasants had already experienced nearly four hundred years of Catholicism, long enough to assimilate it, resist it, and at times transform it. The small figure on the flower vendor's bucket was El Santo Niño, the oldest Catholic icon venerated today in the Philippines. When Magellan hit the archipelago, he was nearing the end of his famed journey, a journey for which he is recognized in history as being the first man to sail around the world, even though he never made it. Before his arrival, the archipelago had been a collection of autonomous and semi-autonomous political and economic organizations. The rajah of Cebu and his queen received Magellan warmly, so warmly that by mid-April, Rajah Humabon, his wives, and subjects became some of the first indigenous Roman Catholic converts when they were baptized by Magellan's priest. Humabon was christened Carlos after Charles I, and Queen Hara became Juana, after Charles's mother. A statue of the Santo Niño was given to Carlos and Juana as a baptismal gift.

Jeremiah and I make our way to the reception hosted by the Filipino writers. We're surprised to see that tents have been set up on the belt of grass near the esplanade, and I feel a slight pinch of guilt at having disparaged the event earlier. The white tents against the now deeper blue of late evening, and the busied glow coming from underneath them is lovely in a way that reminds me of a wedding. We manage to slip in without anyone noticing we're late. We're already drunk, so when plates of lechón, one of the national dishes of the Philippines, are put in front of us we immediately begin shoveling forkfuls of the steaming pork into our mouths. When we're done we're invited to go up for more, which I oblige. The whole spit-roasted pig is on the table, two slits run down both sides of its spine from which the guests have taken most of their meat and left caverns of white sinew underneath the brittle caramel skin. Its face points out toward the reception and looks calm, as though the animal were soundly sleeping. Lechón, and other whole beasts with intact faces, were not unfamiliar to me as food. Lechón, in particular, was familiar in a roundabout way. Even though it's eaten in parts of Mexico, my dad has always avoided eating pork because of a personal paranoia about pork and brain parasites, and my mom tended to avoid all kinds of meat until she eventually stopped eating it entirely when I was a teenager. The first time I'd tried lechón had been at a Puerto Rican neighbor's backyard barbeque, and I later had it again when a Cuban restaurant opened near our home.

No one has touched the poor animal's face. I know that if I dig my thumb into its cheek, where the opening of the lip ends, and tear upward toward its ear I'd get, arguably, the best part. North Americans tend to like the belly, for obvious reasons, but the face of most animals, including pig, lamb, goat, and certain kinds of fish, is, in my opinion, much better. If the pig is properly spit-roasted—meaning that it has taken an absurd amount of time, been brined, and been cared for with frequent basting—the cheek with skin, ear, and fatty tragus contains in one small portion the best of what the whole pig has to offer. The cheek meat will be among the most succulent despite not being heavily marbled (because of the abundance of connective tissue and collagen in this part of the animal), the skin will be brittle like the properly caramelized top of crème brûlée, the tragus will be a sticky, salty bite, and the ear will provide an almost obscene crunch.

The cheek is mine because the Filipino writers have graciously let their guests have first go at the hog, and none of their guests have wanted to eat the face.

By the time we've finished dinner it's dark. Looking out over the water a yellow moon and its reflection look like the jaundiced eyes of a supine stranger. A stage has been set up on the esplanade, and a succession of Filipino poets read their work. I trail off thinking about what my friend said before the trip, about being liked because I looked like a Filipino celebrity, more European, less indigenous, and how much this kind of thing has probably helped me in life. As I watch another poet take the stage, I think about how one reconciles loving oneself as a colonized person.

No matter how much I drink there is always a full sweaty bottle of San Miguel in front of me. I excuse myself to smoke a cigarette underneath a palm tree, and when I stand up I unintentionally pivot backward on my left heel and stumble onto the guest sitting next to me. I'm good and drunk, and when I take the first drag of my cigarette, blinking lights bleed in from my periphery like when you stand up too quickly. I feel a weightlessness that makes me lose awareness of where my limbs are in space, and when I look down at my hand it seems like it can almost be not mine.

The rest of the night's edges blend into one another. After the readings there are a series of cultural performances that feel familiar but distinct. A young boy, maybe six or seven years old, stands in front of the crowd holding two metal orbs of some kind. A woman approaches him and sets them on fire. With his arms limp, he releases the orbs and violently turns his body. They fall until they stop and are revealed to be on chains, and then he swings them in large graceful circles by violently jerking his torso in different directions and at different angles. When the orbs are behind his back they silhouette his small head in a crown of orange fire, and when they come within an inch of his face I can see that he's perfectly calm but looking somewhere else. The more violently he swings his small frame, the hotter the fires burn because of the way wind speaks to fire.

Resistance movements—especially indigenous, ethnic, and religious ones—are often discussed in terms of rejection: rejection of modernity, Western values, and, in the case of the Philippines, Catholicism. But resistance has historically been shaped by the particularities of the aggressors. On Negros, Papa Isio's peasant revolt was shaped by the plantation-like structures of exploitative labor. And long before him, when the Spanish were beginning their conquest, lands and peoples that had previously had little amiable interaction, if any at all, suddenly found themselves banding together against their European attackers. Papa Isio, who became the leader of the fiercest peasant revolt in the Visayas, was a babaylan, a pre-Hispanic figure in Southeast Asian culture that has always served as a medium between realms of indigenous reality, a spiritual guide, political and military leader, and healer. By Papa Isio's time, babaylanism had incorporated Catholic iconography and mythology into its beliefs and practices. Concomitantly, Filipino Catholics had incorporated many pre-Hispanic animistic features into their enactments of faith. In his campaign biography, US-backed Filipino dictator Ferdinand Marcos, who presented himself as the devoutly Catholic leader of Asia's only Christian nation, included the story of how a legendary babaylan made an incision in his back and inserted a petrified wood amulet that gave him the ability to disappear and reappear at will and bring the dead back to life.

The following day comes in short bursts of lucidity. The previous evening ended, or more accurately, didn't end, with a few of us hopping on a motorized tricycle and going to several outdoor bars, and then even fewer of us going back to someone's room at the religious hostel and drinking hot Tanduay from the bottle until the sun peered through the curtains.

When we noticed it was morning, Henry, an American poet with a violently affirmative character, produced an orange prescription bottle.

"This will help us," he said, tipping several peach-colored oval pills into his hand.

Henry's head is a collection of loose curls, and in the neon tube light it looks like a cloud illuminated from within. I open my palm and a cadre of tiny oval pills is there. I stare at him blankly, feeling as though the room were gently swaying. He mumbles something I don't understand, opens the door, and disappears around a corner.

I give my bag to a harbor worker who throws it onto a cart that will be loaded onto the hydrofoil in front of us. I don't remember packing it or recall the bus ride here. Someone shows me a photo of Henry passed out on the bus and a few of me slumped over in several locations taken earlier that day. In one, my eyes are open and looking at the camera but completely vacant, like doll eyes. Because the picture was snapped so recently, looking at it feels like looking into a mirror at someone else. I don't remember being in these moments, and I wonder who it was looking out through my eyes at the world when that photo was taken. I ask Jeremiah if I'd been okay, wondering if I'd managed to keep things together enough for others not to notice what state I was really in, and he said he'd seen me carry on conversations with prestigious Filipino poets, individuals appointed to national councils, and editors of highly circulated magazines, and that I somehow kept track of my own belongings as we switched several modes of transport.

I fall asleep in my window seat on the hydrofoil, and the moment I wake up I'm looking at something that doesn't make sense, so for a few moments I think I'm still asleep. I turn to see if anyone else is looking, and the entire hull of people is turned toward me staring out at the same monstrous thing in absolute silence. The sky is one dark gray mass that looks much thicker than a cloud, almost like smoke that's being drawn downward in a slowly spinning funnel that seems to be depositing the sky into the ocean. I can't tell how close this thing is, so I don't know if I should be worried about dying. I press my palm against the window, but there is no rumbling, just the image. Looking at it in this chemically induced calm makes the dread sink beyond the immediacy of sensation, of panic. It becomes a muted but seething terror at the waterspout, at the randomness of this kind of violence.

Natural disasters and the random, arbitrary death that comes in their wakes fit comfortably within the way we'd like to think the universe is ordered. They provide a template for how we talk about and deal with one kind of atrocity.

Today much of the violence that results from order has been ascribed the inevitability that rightly only belongs to nature, and the institutions that perpetrate it have enough inertia to seem like mountains or tectonic plates. But even in natural disasters, the susceptibility to devastation, the ability to mitigate that devastation, and the ability to better survive it are distributed inequitably. What happens before and after the storm, and to whom? How many bodies are erroneously attributed to the water and the wind?

We arrive in Siquijor somewhat intact and are taken to a rural jungle area to meet with a medicine woman. Later, people will tell me there was a long hike, during which we passed a waterfall and took photographs, but I only remember our arrival at this woman's stilt house, which is among a few other structures built in a clearing. It's surrounded by palm trees and thick green vines that seem to be on the brink of reclaiming the space as jungle. A pale yellow hen pecks around the ground, followed closely by her brown chicks. The medicine woman invites us into the main area of her bamboo structure where there is a single chair in the middle of the room. In the various distinct Filipino cosmologies, spirits are not always benevolent. She tells us, through an interpreter, that she is able to sense when someone has been cursed and that she can lift this curse. One of the group's leaders volunteers, and the old woman tells him to sit. He does, and she walks around him several times, running her hands around his body, never making contact. She stops and says he has had a great curse put upon him. She takes a glass of water that had been on her windowsill and brings her face near the back of the cursed man's head. She breathes in deeply and exhales through a straw into the glass of water, which turns black.

Siquijor is as far south as we'll go. Our conspicuous American presence may not be as welcome any farther south. There are several ongoing conflicts between the government

of the Philippines and Islamic rebel groups seeking autonomy from the state on the southern island of Mindanao.
When the Spaniards arrived in the sixteenth century, they
encountered various distinct ethnolinguistic groups living in
their own political and economic formations in the southern part of the archipelago. The Spaniards called all of them
Moros because they reminded them of their own Moors,
and by the end of the sixteenth century, Spain began sending
military expeditions into the Moro Sultanates. Popular folk
histories characterize this period as one of consistent and
universal resistance to the Spanish crown by Filipino Mus-
lims, but the historical record indicates a more complicated
period marked as much by accommodation to colonial power
as by violent resistance.

I have a few hours of sustained cognizance in the late
afternoon, and somehow the hangover I'd been expecting
never comes. I fall asleep on the bus, and when I wake up
we're unloading near an old Spanish cathedral that would
look abandoned if not for the well-advertised gift shop next
to it. The structure is small, and we're told it dates back to
the late nineteenth century. The white façade is covered in
the black and green stains that accumulate on porous walls
in tropical climates, and it looks like it could cave in without
much force. Inside, the waning sun cuts through stained glass
windows that have been replaced many times, casting colorful geometry on the dirty tile floor. The sensation of déjà vu
overtakes me for a moment as I look at the plaster icons, all
white faces, contorted in agony, looking upward. I've always
wondered where these icons come from, and, operating under the assumption that worshipping unseen gods does not
automatically make someone unreasonable, I've wondered
how these white European faces persist. The Santo Niño
de Cebu is covered in elaborate royal silks and jewels wor-
thy of a king, even though by Christianity's own accounts,
the blessed child was born in a manger to a carpenter and

a homemaker. The cathedral looks like every other Catholic ruin in the so-called Third World. It doesn't seem unlike the cathedral in Fortín.

Outside there is a long iron stand where one can light a votive for a loved one. The candles are all different colors, and when they melt they drip their bright wax over the iron lip onto the ground, where it accumulates into a huge rainbow mass. After the church closes someone must scrape the iron and ground underneath, and the spent wax must be dealt with in some way to make room for tomorrow's candles. I wonder whether it's simply thrown away. Nearby, a child, maybe three or four years old, sits on a curb playing with something in his small hands. I wander over to him because it seems, at first, like he's alone. As soon as I near him, though, the street vendor who'd been stationed on the front sidewalk has turned and is watching me. I smile and nod, and he smiles back. The child looks up and shows me the small matchbox he'd been playing with. He slides it open and a thick black spider with blade-like legs pokes half its body out, and then it fully emerges to crawl around his hands as he laughs.

A few days later, our minders set us loose in Manila, and Jeremiah and I decide to wander around the city on foot without any destination in mind. After a long trek away from our posh hotel, through streets choked with trikes and lined with tall residential towers, we find our way into an area of densely packed buildings that aren't high-rises or newly erected condominiums. It feels like an actual neighborhood. A few kids kick a soccer ball against a tin gate. A woman hangs clothes on a line in a gangway between buildings. A man pulls up to a small grocery store on a bicycle with a large cart platform welded to the front. It's stacked about five feet high with what looks like thousands of eggs, and when he steps on his brakes they come sliding forward off the platform and onto the ground. A deluge of clear and yellow goo

runs down the street. The grocer, an older woman wearing a
blue dress and apron and brown rubber sandals, runs out to
help the poor man salvage some of his eggs, while a few stray
cats lap yolks out of the gutter.

We wander for a few hours turning randomly down residential streets. Jeremiah is a good companion because he is as
keen on getting lost and not talking as I am. Intermittently,
and silently, he points at something he thinks I should see: a
pink furry streak on the asphalt that had once been a kitten,
a sign on a wall for legislation to outlaw the birth control
pill, a small white duck with yellow feet waddling down a
sidewalk as though it were running late for an appointment.
Morning becomes noon and we can feel our scalps burning, so we decide to have lunch in the first place we see. As
we cross the street toward a small outdoor restaurant, I hear
the slapping of footsteps running toward us, and before we
have time to think, there are two children, a girl and a boy,
wrapped around us, begging for money in a few broken English phrases. Neither of us had seen them coming. The sound
of accelerating footsteps coming up behind us had produced
a ball in my throat, and my heart is still pumping so hard it
feels as though something is slamming against my breast-
plate. The girl, maybe five or six, with a long black ponytail
that goes down past her waist, has Jeremiah's arm in a tight
hug, and the boy, around the same age, has all four limbs
fastened around my leg. After I've processed that they're just
children, I let out a breath I didn't realize I'd been holding.
Our first reaction, which is to play with them, comes spon-
taneously, out of sheer astonishment and not knowing what
else to do. Jeremiah gently begins swinging the young girl,
lifting her off the ground, smiling, trying to get her to smile
back. I look down at the boy, whose left eye is completely
red with blood. He's barefoot, they both are, and even from
above I can see thickened, cracked toes and soles from walking the streets without shoes. I puff out my lips and cross my

eyes, which he can't help but laugh at. Their clothes are torn and dirty, and they look malnourished. Jeremiah tells them in English that they need to let go of our arms so we can reach into our pockets, but they either don't understand or don't trust that we'll give them something if they do. We walk a few paces, pulling them along with us, and they continue laughing until we're in front of a 7-Eleven. Abruptly, they bolt away, sprinting across the street, disappearing around a corner. When we turn to look at what they'd seen, there's a guard standing in the window with his hand resting on the grip of a shotgun.

After this we both need beer. We sit under a red San Miguel umbrella in an outdoor restaurant decorated with hanging statues of pink cherubs trailing white ribbons. After our first beer, we decide we need another, and then another. We drink them fast, sitting silently in the shade for some time, not knowing what to say. After a while, I notice that almost everything around us—the napkin holders, the plastic tablecloths, the umbrella casting its red shade—reads *San Miguel.* I was under the impression it was a beer company, but later I'd learn it's the Philippines' largest corporation and has crept into energy, mining, infrastructure, and telecommunications, even a brief stint in commercial air travel. Its chairman, Eduardo Murphy Cojuangco Jr., advised US-backed dictator Ferdinand Marcos through the period of martial law from 1972 until 1981. After Marcos fell out of favor with the United States and fled the Philippines, Cojuangco transitioned into the public sector. At one point, it is estimated, his business empire accounted for one-quarter of the Filipino gross national product. Somehow the ubiquity of the brand name had escaped me until then, but once I was aware of it I saw it everywhere.

On our walk back to our hotel I thought about how transition and continuity are indistinguishable here. The historical sites we'd visited until then had been, if not aseptic, then old enough for spilled blood to have gone cold. They'd been presented to us as historical, that is, they'd performed their historicity by being designated historical sites, relics of a dead and hermetically sealed past. They were set apart from the spaces and time in which they existed, so as tourists we were not obliged to consider the barefoot children in relation to the cathedrals, and the cathedrals in relation to the high-rises and banks. We weren't pressed to follow the gradient from the Spanish crown to American imperialism to our so-called soft power and cronies and corporations. The clipped official histories printed on plaques and materials for guided tours gave us the illusion of being observers, not participants.

We finish our beers and settle up because we have to meet the group for a tour of Intramuros, the walled city that served as the seat of government for the Spanish empire. On our walk back to the hotel we pass a neighborhood of houses made of scrap pieces of wood, corrugated tin, and cardboard. In the window of one there's a young boy, maybe four, leaning his head out, watching the cars go by.

In January 1898, Theodore Roosevelt, then assistant secretary of the navy under President William McKinley, wrote a letter to his brother-in-law in which he lamented "the queer lack of imperial instinct that our people show." He, like many others in Washington, had his "imperial instinct" aroused in the US war with Spain and the possibility of acquiring former colonial possessions. Roosevelt became a leading voice in the push toward expansion in the Pacific as the natural extension of manifest destiny. There were all manner of political philosophies revived or constructed to justify this lust, including political gravitation, natural right, and natural growth. Despite popular resistance to the spirit sweeping Washington, the United States annexed the Philippines in 1899. When anti-imperialists pointed out that spreading the "empire of liberty" by force violated the core principle of "consent of the governed," written in the Declaration of Independence, Roosevelt pointed out that no "sane man" would think this was meant to apply to savages.

The walls of Intramuros are stained with patches of green moss that crawl up and over their highest points. Traffic flows down wide streets that run through openings in forty-foot-thick walls. The fortification is a collage of power and conflict, at times having been occupied, destroyed, rebuilt, and refortified by different belligerents fighting for different interests: landmass, regional control, and domination of trade routes. It has a different quality than the other ruins we've visited thus far, because it's functional and currently transited by locals making their way through Metro Manila.

While we're waiting for the horse-drawn carriages that will take us on our guided tour, I overhear a young boy speaking to his mother in a language I don't recognize before he switches midsentence to nearly unaccented English. Dressed in designer clothing, the mother holds a familiar brown leather purse covered in L's and V's. His quick bouncing between languages reminds me how it would be nearly impossible to find a place in which I couldn't make myself understood in English, about the power and prohibition that comes with speaking or not speaking one of these dominant global languages, and about how enduring the story of the shibboleth has been in our societies.

The boy had also reminded me of myself because of the way he switched languages with ease. He held his mother's hand, and his small voice quickly bounced through syllables. But the language he'd started with wasn't European. It confronted me with the reality that *I* only spoke the languages imposed by two kinds of conquest, and part of that violence had found its way into every aspect of my being: my culture, my speech, my very genetic makeup. Even the voice I hear in my head, the language in which I dream, the way the world is formulated as it passes through my perception, bears those marks.

The carriages pull up, and we're loaded on. I'd thought someone would be guiding our tour with commentary but am pleased to find our carriage ride is silent. The walls of Intramuros have seen waves of violence from different sources, and now they attract tourists to the walled city. After the settler colonialism that had claimed the so-called New World, this seems to have been the first location upon which the United States projected itself imperially, this occupation of an already occupied capital city. Historians disagree about what Thomas Jefferson meant when he formulated America as an "empire of liberty," but the annexation of the Philippines through the abject horrors of war, the immeasurable amount of blood spilled in the process, is another example of why his intent was irrelevant, his words empty. Near the Puerta Isabel II, an entrance and exit in the walled city named after a nineteenth-century Spanish queen, there are the familiar green plastic letters that spell out "Starbucks Coffee" on a wall that bears the ghosts of some of the most brutal history of our past.

Later that evening, after not being able to stop thinking about Intramuros, I slip into a torpor that clouds my thoughts. I lie on the large king-size bed in the sleek hotel suite in which Jeremiah and I are rooming, feeling uneasy. I decide to go for a walk to try to clear my mind, but it takes me about an hour to pry myself from the dim room. As I exit the hotel there are people eating dinner outdoors on elegantly stark tables that run along the exterior. I light a cigarette, and a tall, lean European man wearing brown suede loafers approaches. He asks me for a cigarette in English spoken with a thick French accent. I ask him how he knew to speak to me in English. He smiles. "Lucky guess."

CHAPTER 7

Ceremony

Returning to the United States after having been gone for over a month is disorienting. It feels like entering a foreign country, but it also feels as though I'd never left. Throughout Southeast Asia I'd had encounters with things that were truly foreign to me—bits of culture that were completely unrecognizable—but they were always set within a periphery that was eerily familiar. In the Philippines the colorful, squat Jeepneys that are everywhere first struck me as wholly Filipino cultural objects until someone pointed out that their name came from the US military Jeep that had become ubiquitous during American aggression and occupation. Many of the first-generation Jeepneys had been tricked-out, military surplus Jeeps that were sold to Filipinos after they'd served their purpose. I'd also gone to Cambodia, and as soon as I deplaned there, I noticed an airport employee walking with a wooden crutch because he was missing his right leg from the knee down. I didn't think anything of it until I arrived at my hotel where there was a young man playing a khim in the lobby. He sat on the floor with his legs pointed behind him, and I almost missed seeing that he too was missing the bottom half of a leg, but his was the left. Somehow the connection evaded me until a few hours later, after a much-needed nap and shower, when I had dinner in the empty hotel restaurant. Sitting in silence at Le Bistrot, I awaited a large platter of escargot, and it wasn't until the waiter, a dark brown Cambodian man in his twenties, set the dish down that I realized that seeing two men with missing bottom extremities had not been a coincidence. I remembered bits of what I knew of the international meddling after Cambodia had gained its independence from France, the series of US bombings during the sixties and seventies, and the rise of the Khmer Rouge. For the rest of the meal I thought about a countryside littered with land mines and mass graves.

Upon landing in the United States I check my email after not having checked it for a couple of weeks. One of the first messages is from my landlord, who'd been collecting my mail while I was gone. He wrote that I'd gotten a certified letter from the Department of Homeland Security, and he wanted to know if he should forward it to my parents' place in Chicago. On my layover I call him and asked him to read it to me, which he does. It contains the details for my oath ceremony, which he says is tomorrow, so after flying from Bangkok to Los Angeles, and then from Los Angeles to Chicago, I borrow a friend's car and take off for Iowa City.

I zone in and out of driving because I haven't slept and there are only intermittent cars after long stretches of nothing. For dozens of miles there is only the rhythm of the yellow lines on the triangles of black asphalt made visible by the headlights. I lose track of the fact I've been driving for long periods, so when I am finally present again it's scary that I don't remember the last ten or twenty minutes of steering the vehicle at eighty miles an hour. I mostly daydream about Iowa, about how strange it is that after having lived in Chicago for over two decades, the place where I'd be naturalized would be West Branch, Iowa, a city with a population of just over two thousand, to which I have never even been. I think about the life-sized butter cow at the Iowa State Fair, about the National Cattle Congress, about politicians making pilgrimages to the heartland for down-home footage, about the Field of Dreams in Dyersville, and about the plaque in Riverside that looks like a headstone and reads "FUTURE BIRTHPLACE OF CAPTAIN JAMES T. KIRK, MARCH 22, 2228." I think about the 2008 Postville Agriprocessors raid, the largest single raid of a workplace in US history to that point, in which a kosher slaughterhouse in northeastern Iowa was stormed by Immigration and Customs Enforcement. Just under four hundred workers were convicted of document fraud and served five months in prison before being deported. I think of the two 25,000-square-foot golden domes of Maharishi University of Management in Fairfield, where hundreds of Iowans attempt to reach enlightenment through the practice of Transcendental Meditation.

I call and leave a message for my Iowa friend Chelsea, asking if I can sleep on her couch because I'd sublet my apartment to a traveling nurse for the summer.

Chelsea calls as I'm passing "the world's largest truck-stop," a four-hundred-parking-spot facility with a chrome and accessory shop for big rigs, two tricked-out semis, a dental clinic, theater, barber, public library, chiropractor, shower facility, and fast-food court. She says she's just landed from her own return trip through Korea, and that I can meet her at her place. As I pull up, her fat white cat jumps out of her roommate's open window and disappears into the neighbor's tall bushes. For a moment I think about climbing in through the window so I can go to sleep but decide it would be dangerous, so I sit on her porch chain-smoking. The eastern Iowa sunset this time of year makes whatever is underneath look picturesque. The intensity of the pinks and oranges seems impossible. On the drive here, the rolling hills really do look as pristine as they look in Grant Wood paintings, and it's very difficult to see why this is a fiction. Peppered along the roads there are long, one-level structures that look like warehouses, with built-in fans down the sides. This is to mitigate the lack of windows. Each is crammed with tens of thousands of chickens that wallow in their own filth and have less than a square foot of space to move for most of their lives. And far from the roads, away from visibility, there are slaughterhouses that are illegal to photograph, staffed by temp agencies that broker undocumented labor.

When I open my eyes the following morning it takes me longer than usual to remember where I am. For a few moments after I raise my head, I think I might still be overseas, but as I examine the objects and furniture in the room—a dream catcher, earrings made of animal bones, a few crystals splayed out on an old wooden desk—I know I'm in the room of a hipster in the United States. I can hear the shower, and I remember that Chelsea had come home with a case of beer and that we'd gone to sleep only very recently. Because of the short notice, my parents weren't able to come for the ceremony, which didn't seem to bother them, so Chelsea said she'd accompany me to take photos. On our way out, our mutual friend Dylan, who grew up in the Alleghenies, shows up wearing a shirt with a collar, which is unusual for him, especially in the summertime. I've forgotten that I'd texted him at some point the previous evening, but it seemed appropriate that this Appalachian friend, the son of a street preacher, would be joining us. I'd lied to both of them, telling them that the ceremony started an hour before it actually did, because I felt confident that something would go wrong.

The first impediment presents itself in the form of a careening semi that comes inches from smashing into my driver's side and runs us off the road. I try not to over-swerve, but we pop onto the shoulder and narrowly miss a concrete embankment. When the car comes to a stop we don't acknowledge how close the bottom edge of the semi's cargo box came to the driver's side windows. We are still and silent for a moment, and then, not knowing what to do or say, I accelerate back into traffic. The female voice on the GPS leads us off the highway into an area with several office parks. Here we encounter our second impediment. The voice tells us we've arrived as we pull into the lot, but there isn't a single vehicle here, only a small, one-level structure at the far end that looks abandoned or at least closed. We park, and, halfway expecting the doors not to open, we go inside. Two old men in guard uniforms are chatting about something and seem surprised to see us. It turns out the woman who I'd spoken with on the phone at USCIS gave me the incorrect address. The older of the two guards checks his watch and informs us that the naturalization ceremony is several towns over, in West Branch, which is about half an hour away. Dylan and Chelsea become agitated, thinking we'll surely miss the appointment, until I tell them we actually have more than enough time.

I have never been to West Branch, Iowa, before, but as we drive down what appears to be the main street, which we later discover is named Main Street, it looks utterly familiar. If not for a few new Camrys and minivans it would be like looking at a photograph from the forties or fifties. Many of the buildings are redbrick with ornate beige cornices and big windows with striped awnings, and one place has a faded US flag flapping in the wind, but several of the storefronts are closed, and there's no one on the street. We pull into the parking lot of what appears to be a small grocery store called Jack and Jill, and I make a comment about how nice it is to see a small independent grocery store still in operation in this small town, but Dylan corrects me, telling me it's a regional chain.

"Besides, most of these people shop at the Walmart in Coralville," he says.

The young woman who checks us out doesn't say a word as she slides our items across the scanner. She just stares at our eyes, smacking her chewing gum, looking uninterested and interested at the same time. She's short and thin and wears a big faded camouflage coat and loose jeans. My ham sandwich is under three dollars. When I open it, the white bread is soaked, either from the shredded iceberg lettuce or the ham. We walk toward the Herbert Hoover Presidential Library and Museum where the two old guards told us the ceremony would take place. Main Street is still empty and the sky looks big, like it's bearing down on buildings that might give under its weight at any moment. We round a corner onto another abandoned street that looks like a period piece film set, but this one appears much older. A weathered white sign reads "Downey Street" in hand-painted old-timey letters. We later learn that this historic-looking street is, in fact, a national historic site and the re-created neighborhood of Herbert Hoover's birth. It's lined with small cottages, a blacksmith shop, an old schoolhouse, a Quaker meeting-house, and the tall native wildflowers and grasses that would have been here in the late nineteenth century. Some of the structures, like the small white cottage where Hoover was born, are only somewhat original. The cottage, for example, had been sold during Hoover's lifetime, a second story had been added, and the cottage had been rotated to face another street, but decades later, after Hoover became president, the cottage was bought back, the second floor removed, and the structure was turned to face Downey Street again for the purposes of historic authenticity.

We stand in front of the birth cottage, at the white pickets that line the small property. Chelsea points out that there's a water pump and pile of firewood in the yard, and Dylan wonders aloud who cuts the grass and whether or not the pump actually produces water. The buildings on the street were never as they are now. They were placed in rows like this to facilitate a "historical" experience, and on some days, some of the locals, who live just blocks over in houses with vinyl siding, are paid to wear bonnets and period clothing and walk around, chop wood, and play games as though it were the late 1800s. The cottage is only fourteen by twenty feet, and it feels like this is what I'm supposed to walk away noting: its modesty. It's strange to think all these little houses sit empty and actors are paid to sometimes pretend to inhabit them. For Hoover, the cottage was "physical proof of the unbounded opportunity of American life," and this is what he tells us his story tells: "In no other land could a boy from a country village, without inheritance or influential friends, look forward with unbound hope." The house isn't lived in and cannot be sold, so its only use is as a tool for myth-making.

As we continue toward the library we come upon a pedestal topped by a seven-foot black statue of a woman sitting on a throne. Her face and body are draped in a thin black veil, giving her an ominous, almost ghoulish appearance. The veil, made of bronze, has been cast to look thin, airy, and somehow light. Her features, although obscured, are still perceptible. The three of us stand at the foot, and Chelsea points to an inscription at the base: "Je suis ce qui a été, ce qui est, et ce qui sera, et nul mortel n'a encore levé le volle qui me couvre." *I am that which was, that which is, and that which will be, and no mortal has yet lifted the veil that covers me.* The figure, cast by Belgian sculptor Auguste Puttemans, is Isis, ancient Egyptian goddess of life and nature, whose name means throne, and whose headdress is often depicted in the shape of a throne. Belgians had meant the statue to be an expression of gratitude to Hoover for famine relief efforts during World War I, because Isis is sometimes used to represent the proliferation of grain, but in Egypt, Isis served primarily as the personification of the pharaoh's power. Three bronze flames emanate from her right hand, and she holds the key of life in her left.

"Weird," says Chelsea, staring at her ghostly features.

This version of Isis, cloaked almost completely, does seem

peculiar. In Plutarch's *Moralia*, there is a reference to a statue of Athena in the ancient city of Saïs that contains a similar inscription: "I am all that has been, and is, and shall be, and my robe no mortal has yet uncovered." Plutarch suggests that the statue of Athena represents the use of myth by the priestly and military classes from which kings were appointed. The cloaking of certain knowledge meant that only some would be privy to it, and so only some would be able to derive benefit from it. Moreover, the identification of Isis with Athena and the sculpture's Greek rather than Egyptian aesthetic bring to mind Athena's associations with courage, law, justice, and war strategy. It seems strangely appropriate on our way to the Hoover Library, then, to encounter this dark figure—cloaked and on her throne, overlooking a presidential birth cottage—like a sphinx at the entrance to the temple.

Inside the library, a young Indian or Pakistani boy, maybe seven years old, stands alone in a corner, pummeling a portable video game with his thumbs. A long single-file line snakes out of the main auditorium, and clusters of family members stand around avoiding eye contact. Chelsea leans toward me to whisper in my ear that the mood isn't as jovial as she'd expected. The kid's device is clinking and pinging, and he thrashes about from time to time. I wonder if he was born here or elsewhere, and, if it's elsewhere, I wonder whether he has any memories of the place of his birth. I wonder how his parents explained this ceremony here today.

It seems significant that after living in Chicago for twenty years I'm being naturalized here, now, under the sign of Obama, the record-breaking deporter in chief, with Hoover, the president during the beginning of the Mexican Repatriation, in retrograde. The walls are covered in photographs showing Hoover's accomplishments. What isn't displayed on the wall, of course, is anything regarding the policy authorized by Hoover that led to the coercive, often violent removal of between four hundred thousand and two million Mexicans living in the United States. Many of whom were US citizens or legal residents whose families hadn't moved in generations and who had only become "foreigners" after the United States invaded Mexico, took half of its landmass, and drew a new political boundary line. This period between 1929 and 1944 shares many similarities to the moment in which we live. And like Operation Wetback in the fifties straight through our current period, the categories of Mexican, immigrant, "illegal immigrant," and "wetback" get ground together in the public consciousness. The xenophobia and racial terror that continues to this day certainly isn't new, and neither is the collective amnesia regarding the economic, political, and military interventionism that has in large part driven migration to the United States.

Chelsea snaps a photo of me standing in front of glass doors etched with the presidential seal. The backlight turns me into a black, featureless silhouette in the center of a ring of stars. My body covers the eagle and the olive branch it clasps in its left talon, but the thirteen arrowheads peek from behind my right elbow and a halo of rays emanates from around my head. The single-file line starts moving so I get in the back, and an attendant comes out to tell everyone's family members they can go into the auditorium and sit down. An older woman wearing a long green sari grabs the kid from the corner who is still pummeling his device. He lets out a grunt when she tugs him by the arm, but otherwise his attention is uninterrupted. She tries to sneak a kiss on his cheek, but he pulls away without turning his gaze from the game.

There's a young black man standing in front of me. The back of his head is dotted with a few small white puffy scars. He turns to wave and smile at an older white couple looking

excitedly at him. They wave back. These have been long journeys, I don't doubt that. Everyone here—everyone in line—
has personal complications, unique thoughts and feelings
regarding what they're about to do or what is about to happen to them. Really it's already done. Many of the families in
the hallway look genuinely excited. One young woman tears
up as she hugs a man who looks like he might be her brother
or maybe her boyfriend. Others look anxious, and a few look
entirely unmoved. One man's relatives stand in complete silence, with no expressions, and don't acknowledge when he
breaks away from them to get into the line.

Many of these trajectories have been labored in ways I'll
never have to know. My own has been rather mild because
my parents bore the brunt of our migration, and I had the
luxury of being too young to remember the place we left. I
can't miss it because I never knew it, so I don't feel the sad-
ness some of them probably do, but it does feel like I've been
denied something essential. I'm a stranger to most of my
blood relatives and not by my own choosing. Neither of the
two languages I speak are indigenous to the place in which
I was born. My parents left a way of life, which means the
way in which they'd grown to relate to the things and people around them, the spaces they had carved out for themselves. They left fathers, mothers, brothers, and sisters. They
left the familiar rhythms of the quotidian in their corner of
the world; the thick loamy smell that came off the mountain
during rain; the sound of crickets landing on the neighbor's
tin roof through an open window; the walk around the park
on Sunday; watching their viejos grow old; being there to
help them die.

When I started the process of "naturalization," feelings
that had abated, that I'd become somewhat accustomed
to, were agitated. A few months back I'd confessed to my
mother that for a long time, maybe always, I'd felt a deep
abiding guilt for being the reason they left everything. With-

out any siblings to shoulder any of this, it fell squarely on me. She sat silent for a long moment, her bottom lip tightening the way it does when she's pained. Then she offered something she knew I would understand to be true, rather than something that sounded nice but wouldn't bring me any solace. She said even if they had stayed, those things would have been taken away, that everything always gets taken away, and that I wasn't the reason why, that the reasons were too many, too complex, too permanent to understand. She said what had happened to them had also happened to me—in my own way—and she'd always worried I might carry this kind of guilt.

The line starts to move and everyone's family is corralled into the auditorium to be seated. We walk toward a stage at the front where four individuals sit at a folding table covered in papers and envelopes. As I'm moving forward I remember a joke Yoli had said about the ceremony, about everyone being handed blond wigs and blue contact lenses as they swore allegiance to the US flag. I knew my parents had wanted to come, but I could also sense they weren't too torn up about not being able to take the time off from work on such short notice. I feel a similar ambivalence about being here without them because being here doesn't feel like a celebration or an accomplishment. It's something of a relief, of course, but it also feels like acquiescence—like I'm tacitly agreeing this is necessary and legitimate, that, yes, in fact, I am one of the "good ones" and I have "done it the right way."

One of the women at the folding table asks me for my letter in the pinched, nasally accent some Iowans have.

"What letter, ma'am?" I ask.

She explains that it said right on the letter that I needed to bring it to the ceremony. I try to explain why I don't have it but only manage a few vowel sounds before she raises her finger—telling me to wait—while she quietly confers with the others at the table. She asks me to step to the side and wait a moment. A man comes from somewhere, and they all quietly confer with him, periodically looking in my direction. The man leaves, and the woman waves me over.

"Okay then. I'll need your green card, and I need you to fill this out."

I hadn't thought about needing my green card, but I have it on me because there is rarely ever a moment when I don't. Printed right on the card is the direction that I'm required to have it with me at all times. For a moment I think about asking if I can keep it, but I don't. She takes it from me and drops it in the "O" section of a small plastic bin on the table. She hands me a clipboard with a form that contains several questions I've already answered. When I'm done she takes it and explains that she just has a few questions she has to ask me.

"Have you been out of the country since the civics interview?"

"Yes."

She looks up from her papers.

"Since the civics interview?"

"Yes."

She leans forward putting some weight on her elbows.

"How long were you continuously out of the country?"

"About a month."

"One month?"

"Yes."

She writes things down on her clipboard, and it seems like I've given her the wrong answer. She grabs a file box and fingers through some papers until she stops at what she's looking for. She pulls out a single sheet of paper and holds it out to me.

"There you are."

For a moment I don't know what I'm looking at. It looks like a giant dollar bill rimmed in the same baroque filigree. There's a passport-size photograph of myself that I don't immediately recognize, with my signature next to it. I stare at it for a moment, and realize, because of the trench coat I'm wearing in it, that it's the photograph that was taken during my biometrics appointment. The woman at the table tells me to sign it, and it's only as I'm signing it that I realize it's my certificate of naturalization. She writes a number, 37, on a small square of paper and tells me to find my seat.

The chairs in the first few rows have large white envelopes with numbers on them. I find 37. The person assigned 36 is not yet to my right, but sitting to my left is 38, an older pale woman with bright orange hair. She keeps turning around to wave at someone, and her perfume overwhelms me every time she does. She's very fidgety and obviously excited, and I know enough about her experience, just because she's number 38, to feel a vague kinship with her. There are several gold rings on each of her fingers, and a thick crucifix is wedged between her breasts.

A bald judge in robes walks in from behind the stage. Eleven middle-aged white men follow him out, wearing red button-down shirts. They assemble into a small semicircle on the left side of the stage, and one man introduces them as members of the Harmony Hawks, a seventy-member barbershop chorus. Several of the men resemble Kenny Rogers, and others have the blunt look of Bavarian stock, all foreheads and thick fingers. The judge reads an introduction, which is really just a list of the requirements we've met in order to be naturalized. They increase in absurdity, reaching an apex when he tells us that we've established our good moral character during the legally mandated statutory period, have demonstrated our attachment to the principles of the US Constitution, and have shown ourselves to be well disposed to the good order and happiness of the United States. We've demonstrated, unless exempt by law, the ability to read, write, and speak words in ordinary usage in the English language. We have demonstrated our understanding of the fundamentals of the history and government of the United States.

There are forty-seven of us. I open my white envelope. Inside is a small US flag made of thin vinyl. There are a few other papers inside that I don't retrieve. Looking around, others have also pulled out their tiny flags, not knowing what we're supposed to do with them. The Harmony Hawks begin "God Bless America" in the hammy barbershop style, which I can usually walk away from if ever confronted with it, but here I'm stuck. The singers smile between phrases, and when they're done they look happily upon the crowd. But any happiness directed toward me, toward us, feels contingent on the fact that we've jumped through the correct hoops.

In today's liberal democratic states a substantial portion of law is dedicated to erecting a "just" basis for exclusion, to pretending that the universal right to leave any country exists when it doesn't. The wealthy, despite their racial identity or country of origin, transcend borders. But here, in the domain of restrictive immigration policy, democracy reaches its vanishing point. Considering the history of colonialism and the continued economic and political force exerted by the global North on the global South, restrictive immigration policy looks more like affluent states shielding themselves against the misery they create elsewhere than anything international jurists could ever come up with. The more I turn these thoughts over in my mind, the more grating the chorus's harmonizing becomes. This is pure spectacle, one in which forty-seven people are offered as proof the system is working, that the spirit of democracy exists for everyone, that human dignity is respected, that inalienable rights are recognized, and that liberty is for all who show up to claim it.

A representative for Iowa congressman Dave Loebsack reads a statement. "You are proof that the American dream is alive and well!" he says. Then there is more singing.

The judge tells us we are not yet citizens, that we'll become citizens the moment we utter the words "I will," affirming our willingness to take up arms and uphold hollow ideals put on paper by people who bought and sold human beings, while our military's drones "legally" rain death from above and violate the sovereignty of other nations, some of whose people are being naturalized here today. The judge reads through each person's country of origin individually: Canada, Eretria, Latvia, China, Montenegro, Pakistan, Romania, the Central African Republic, Bolivia, Vietnam, China, India, Kosovo, Pakistan, Pakistan, Pakistan, Nigeria, Mexico, Vietnam, the Philippines, Sweden, Somalia, Jamaica, Venezuela, Kenya, Poland, Liberia, Vietnam, Algeria, Canada, Ukraine, Bosnia, Ukraine, South Korea, Bosnia, India, Mexico, Latvia, the Philippines, Mexico, India, Sri Lanka, India, Bosnia, Sri Lanka, Togo, South Korea. I think the young man with the scars on his head is Liberian, and the woman with the bright orange hair to my left is from Latvia. Number 36 to my right is a small man with dark brown skin from India who turns and smiles at me when the judge reads India, and the kid who was pummeling the game in a corner belongs to a family from Pakistan.

We all raise our right hands. The judge reads his prompt. We each say, "I will."

The lights grow dim and a video is projected on a screen onstage. Barack Obama, presumably somewhere in the White House, looks just above and beyond us because he's not looking into the camera but at cue cards or a teleprompter just to the side.

"I am proud to welcome you as a new citizen of the United States of America."

How strange to be welcomed now, since I've lived my life here from before I can remember. My cultural references are decidedly eighties and nineties United States—Urkel, Alex P. Keaton, *Tom & Jerry*, Biggie—and despite my best efforts I sometimes slip into a Chicago accent, cutting my

A's short. When I did visit Veracruz as a middle-schooler, the kids I played pickup games of soccer with would immediately detect that something about me was off. I had my first kiss in a bathroom in Bucktown in Chicago in grammar school, and I lost my virginity less than a block away in a church parking lot. The first place I remember living was a yellow brick apartment building across the street from Holstein Park on the corner of Shakespeare and Oakley. The super had plaque psoriasis and lived on the ground floor, and I used to think he was related to me somehow because he was always around. My dad saved my life when he tackled me on Palmer walking toward Western—we'd gotten caught between two teenagers shooting at each other. I wrecked the first car my parents ever bought three days after they'd made the last payment, crossing North Avenue on Honore.

I don't feel any different after saying "I will," but I know there are some real changes that have just taken place, not to my body—and it's really too soon for anything to have changed in my mind—but to the relations I have to the place in which I live, its bureaucracy, and its ability to restrict my movement. The virtual me—constructed and siphoned from various sources of data—will be transmitted across their interlinked databases differently, coded differently. The list of potential punishments for my actions has been reconfigured and shrunk. I've been allowed to join the club, brought into new spheres of influence and slipped out of others, and all in one breath. It isn't lost on me that people die in pursuit of this condition I've just entered.

The official Customs and Border Protection number of migrants' lives lost in the Southwest during fiscal year 2010 is 365. This number is almost certainly too low. The number of South and Central American migrants killed in their transit through Mexico on their way here is unknown. Migrant massacres numbering close to one hundred are not uncommon. Falling off the side of La Bestia, a freight train used for transport through Mexico, and never being identified is not uncommon. About eleven thousand South and Central American migrants were kidnapped in a six-month period last year. Globally thousands of people perish making this wager, attempting to make their way to the global North. They die in the Sahara, along the US-Mexico border, in Mexico, in the Mediterranean, in Australian waters, around the Horn of Africa, in the Bay of Bengal, and in the Caribbean. They are the poorest, those who cannot afford to make their way into a country on a tourist visa or on an airplane. Many come from indigenous populations. Most are dark-skinned.

The ceremony in West Branch, Iowa, reaches its nadir when a video is cued up and a twangy guitar or maybe synthesizer begins Lee Greenwood's "God Bless the USA." A video montage that reminds me of every propaganda film I've ever seen begins diffusing cliché images intended, I suppose, to kick-start our patriotism for the new homeland: a snow-capped mountain, a swooping helicopter shot of a golden field of grain, a bald eagle soaring above a forest, a roaring river, a flag undulating in the sky. Usually I would find this comical, but about halfway through I feel a shudder. This song had been playing a lot on the radio lately, and I've come to find out that it was originally popular as US-led coalition forces dropped ninety thousand tons of bombs during the Gulf War. It became popular again just after Operation Enduring Freedom (Afghanistan) and Operation Iraqi Freedom, and it's in the middle of a resurgence that started a little over a month ago when Beyoncé premiered her cover on *Piers Morgan Tonight*, three nights after the assassination of Osama bin Laden. The song reminds me not only of the televised images I'd seen during my childhood of Kuwait on fire, but also of the drunken crowds I recently saw taking to the streets in the small Iowa city in which I live. At first I didn't know what was happening because

I didn't own a television, and I assumed it had something to do with football, but my neighbor knocked on my door to tell me the news. Crowds of drunken college students and locals spilled out of apartment buildings, frat houses, and bars onto the streets. It looked exactly the same as the white rioting that happens when the football team wins, except instead of black-and-gold banners they were waving the stars and stripes and chanting "U-S-A! U-S-A! U-S-A!" Rather than celebrating a sporting victory, though, they were in ecstasy over the revenge assassination of Osama bin Laden, which we would later come to learn allegedly happened in front of his twelve- or thirteen-year-old daughter.

Without a trace of self-awareness, the old white judge tells us that America is the home of immigrants: "Baryshnikov, the dancer; Einstein, the scientist; Alexander Graham Bell, the inventor; Wayne Gretzky, the hockey player." I retrieve a handful of papers from inside my large white envelope. The first sheet is a form letter from Obama. I skim it as the judge announces he'll be taking photographs with people on stage. I glance over, and number 38 is wiping away a tear. *"You're one of us now"*—this is the overwhelming sentiment of the letter. A woman who's just been naturalized takes her whole family up for a photo: several children, a husband, and a baby. The judge holds the baby—his idea. Something falls from the papers I'm holding onto the ground. It's a government-printed informational pamphlet about applying for a US passport. The front reads, "With Your U.S. Passport, the World is Yours!"

CHAPTER 8

Friendship Park, USA

Over my left shoulder is a series of rolling hills that look like brown waves frozen mid-swell. The highest one spits out Border Patrol vehicles that pop over the horizon and then kick up clouds of dirt as they wind down the road toward me. To my right is a desolate beach—not a soul on it except someone inside a green-and-white Border Patrol Jeep parked on the wet sand where there should be children digging holes or building castles.

In front of me is an iron fence, about twenty feet high, which extends several hundred feet in each direction. This barrier fences off another fence, about the same height, made of rusted iron beams that bifurcate the rolling hills and extend into the Pacific Ocean. It looks like a spine protruding from a giant rotting fish. All of the standard reasons given for erecting such a thing become suspect after even the most cursory investigation. I'm standing directly in front of the only entrance to the area between the two fences, which may or may not be part of Friendship Park. About twenty feet over my left shoulder is a Border Patrol SUV, motor running, angled diagonally so its front is pointing at the entrance like a hunting dog pointing at game.

I'm not entirely sure what constitutes Friendship Park, because nothing here looks park-like or friendly. The sky

is gray but also somehow bright. Things look crisp but ane-
mic, glaring but drained of color. It's as if the sun itself is
emitting gray. This corner of the nation resembles a cleared
prison yard or a camp. It looks like a ruined Tarkovskian
landscape: the rusted wall that extends past the horizon, the
lone beach with the solitary vehicle, the conspicuous absence
of people. A lopsided sign on the first fence reads "THIS
AREA UNDER 24 HOUR SURVEILLANCE." I snap a
photo just as a wad of white seagull shit plops on the concrete next to me. Somehow I'd missed seeing the eighty-foot
surveillance tower just a few hundred feet away where a few
fat gulls squawk, perched on the edges of a triangular catwalk
beside infrared cameras and ground surveillance radar.

Nothing about the infrastructure here makes clear sense.
It's well documented, for example, that the crime rate among
foreign-born and first-generation immigrants is much lower
than the crime rate of the US-born population. Studies
suggest "second-generation immigrants" assimilate precipi-
tously, and their experiences are shaped by the same vulnerabilities, influences, and temptations as other Americans,
so their crime rates "catch up" to those of native-born non-
Hispanic white people. "Second-generation immigrants" is
itself a misleading designation, because people in this category aren't immigrants at all but persons born in the United
States to at least one immigrant parent. In any case, there is
no evidence to suggest that the fortification at this boundary
diminishes illegal entry into the United States in any way.
More accurately, it displaces it.

"This is creepy," says my partner, Caitlin, scanning the
landscape. She says she's a bit ashamed she's never been here
before, because she grew up in Escondido, only about forty-
five minutes north of here, but I tell her that even if she had
come it wouldn't have been *this* place exactly, because until
2009 it still looked like something that could pass for a park.

On our drive here we had talked about how it seemed that a significant part of what shapes immigrant experience is the premise that immigration is a single issue rather than matrixes of issues with distinct contexts and various scales. Caitlin had accused me of being grumpy, and I'd responded by asking her if she knew how many of Mexico's recent heads of state were Harvard and Yale grads. I borrowed her iPhone and pulled up a photo my cousin had recently posted on Facebook of my elderly great aunt. I showed her the photo and told her it was my Tía Elena who lived in Fortín, and I showed her the location my cousin added to the post, which read: "Walmart—México." The photo was a full body shot of an elderly, light brown woman wearing a cardigan and an ankle-length skirt, standing in front of an out-of-focus shelf. Much of the blurry area in the frame was taken up by blue rectangles from Walmart aisle signage.

"Jesus," she said.

The fact that we could re-create an almost identical image less than five miles from our Iowa City apartment meant there were many kinds of migration taking place.

As we traveled down the highway I found myself mindlessly repeating the word "Escondido" the way Caitlin said it, *Ehs-cun-dee-doh*. Most of the street names, town names, city names, and names of natural features were all in Spanish here, for obvious reasons—something I already knew—but until I repeated the word over and over, the meaning, *the hidden one*, hadn't registered. I thought about how since yesterday, when we arrived in Solana Beach to visit her parents, I'd been reading street signs and hearing names, all Spanish words, but none of their actual meanings were carried by the utterances I heard: sun trap, solarium, the hidden one, ranch of little bluffs, the jewel, the drawer, the sea, knoll of holy faith, the king, the golden one.

Yesterday evening Caitlin and I took her parents' dog on

a walk down their block, passing lovely ranch-style homes nestled behind hedges and hills covered in ice plants. The block descends to an entrance for the San Elijo Lagoon, a wildlife preserve and estuary. We followed the trail for a minute or so before it opened to a sprawling wet valley of intense greens and dark shallow ponds that reflected the pink sky. It seemed impossible something like it could be there just at the end of their residential street. One white egret stood motionless, not rippling the oval of water it was standing in, and a lean white arrow streaked across the horizon, diminishing upward into the distance. We continued winding through the trails where the occasional jogger trotted past us, nodding or saying hello.

As I sipped coffee the following morning, the tranquility I still felt from the estuary was disrupted when two Mexican men walked into the backyard carrying work gear. Caitlin, her mom, and I had been chatting casually, puttering around the kitchen, which looks out onto the backyard. When the men appeared, the room tightened. Caitlin's eyes were fixed on mine, and I could tell she didn't want to turn to see the men, even though she'd already seen them in her periphery. Her mom busied herself wiping the counters, avoiding eye contact with us both. We spent a few hard seconds locked in place like this until I excused myself to go to the bathroom. When I came back, they'd both gone into their bedrooms to get ready for the day. I finished the rest of my coffee standing at the window, wondering what I would do when one of the men looked over and saw me, but that moment never came.

Afterward I felt a tinge of foolishness for having allowed myself to be lulled by the serenity of the morning, the lushness of the estuary. An awareness of myself in relation to this place was brought back by the men and the feeling that materialized in the room when we all saw them. If I were to walk out to the first intersection, and turn down any street I would pass homes worth over a million dollars, even in this cold market, and chances are I wouldn't see anyone who looked like me unless they were doing work, because despite California being populated by so many brown people, this enclave's population is 85.8 percent white. And just beyond the estuary's eastern horizon are the mansions of Rancho Santa Fe, the zip code with the highest percentage of million-dollar homes in the entire country. The marsh itself is an accessory, a place for these people's leisure activities. I doubt any of the men who arrive in work trucks full of gear have ever stepped foot in it. I wouldn't go in it alone without a white person by my side, or at least a leashed dog.

When Caitlin returned the two men were gone. We didn't acknowledge the incident, but there was a period of tense silence between us in the car as we drove toward Friendship Park in her parents' old Mercedes wagon. We'd met in a dingy bar in Iowa City called George's Buffet. And after our first encounter I found myself doodling the shape of her smile—a scalene triangle with the longest side up—in my notebooks. I remember Googling her a day or two after we met and finding a recording of her reading two of her poems. Most of the other writers I'd met in Iowa City struck me as overprivileged children playing at making meaning or resisting it by performing irony and other affects. After hearing her read her work I wanted to know her. I'd just broken up with my previous girlfriend of a decade because I'd slept with another woman and in doing so realized I was trying to ensure the dissolution of our relationship. I didn't want a life of acquiring and maintaining comfort, which is what it would have been. When I heard Caitlin's poems I imagined an unruly person who wouldn't be able to fit into any of the regular schemes life tends toward today. I was in love with her after only a week.

• • •

A line of gray pelicans glides low over the double barrier and then out and over the Pacific. A few rays of sun have managed to burn through the marine layer and fall on the hulking rusted wall, making it look for a moment like the edge of a forest fire.

On August 18, 1971, First Lady Pat Nixon was photographed in this very spot, laughing nervously and somewhat coquettishly beside a shirtless, long-haired surfer. In the photo, she's wearing a white skirt suit with overlaid white circles, and just beyond her bouffant is a view of the bull-fighting ring in Tijuana where fights were telecast to Los Angeles and called in English on radio simulcast by Sidney Franklin, the first successful Jewish-American bullfighter from Brooklyn. A crowd of Mexicans stands behind a few strands of barely visible barbed wire to watch the first lady plant a tree to inaugurate the park. After saying a few words, a member of her security detail led her to a section where the wire had been clipped. She crossed the international boundary line and shook hands with bell-bottomed Mexicans, and she embraced some of their children for photographs. "I hate to see a fence anywhere," she said. "I hope there won't be a fence here too long."

For many years it was barbed wire, and then I read somewhere that what went up during Operation Gatekeeper in 1994 were welded metal landing mats from old aircraft carriers used in the Vietnam and Gulf wars. The year of Gatekeeper was also the year of NAFTA (the North American Free Trade Agreement), so in Mexico, as the local was exposed to the pressures of the global, and as so-called structural adjustment displaced people, restrictions on movement increased. After 9/11 the manufactured threat of terrorism coming across the southern border brought "immigration" under the rhetorical dominion of national security rather than just criminality and economics. And today the erecting of this infrastructure is investable. Private firms compete for public contracts because carving out a place in the border security industry is increasingly lucrative. The 2013 "immigration reform" bills proposed by the House of Representatives (H.R. 1417) and the Senate (S. 744) are different in many ways, but they share the same border security paradigm: to achieve "situational awareness" of the entire Southwest border, which means 100 percent surveillance, and to maintain "operational control," meaning that at the very least 90 percent of unauthorized entries must be deterred. These are unprecedented goals in our North American context.

The major difference in the proposals is the Senate bill uses some of the enforcement benchmarks as "triggers" for initiating immigration relief for many of the undocumented individuals already in country. This ties the benefits of in-country migrant groups to the detriment—in many cases fatal—of individuals in earlier stages of very similar migrations. This macabre knot was regarded as the more liberal of the two bills because the House proposal is an enforcement-only bill, meaning it contains no immigration relief whatsoever. The Senate bill, if signed into law, would have allocated $46.3 billion for Southwest border enforcement whether or not it was necessary, in addition to the $100 billion the United States has already burned through in border security. In his article "The Green Monster," for *Politico Magazine*, journalist Garrett M. Graff points out the United States already "spends more money each year on border and immigration enforcement than the combined budgets of the FBI, ATF, DEA, Secret Service and U.S. Marshals—plus the entire NYPD annual budget." If signed into law, S. 744 would have nearly doubled the number of deployed full-time Border Patrol agents, bringing the total to 38,405. It would have added 3,500 Customs and Border Protection officers, funded the erecting of seven hundred additional miles of fencing, and purchased and deployed enough surveillance watch towers, camera systems, seismic sensors, drones, mobile surveillance systems, and the like to attempt to reach 100 percent surveillance.

The bill was passed in June 2013 by the Senate in a vote of 68–32, but as of fall 2015 the House had refused to consider it.

A kid I remember named James might have been my first white friend. He lived two buildings down and was one of the only white kids in the neighborhood. We got along great because he always wanted to play Twenty-one, and so did I. I don't remember much about our friendship, because I was only seven when I knew him, but I know things were uncomplicated because we were too young for them to be, and because he lived two doors down in a building like ours with his Polish grandmother. Kids in the neighborhood called him James, sometimes "White Boy," but nobody cared that he was white because he sank everything from the three-point line. One of the only clear memories I have about him was the time his grandmother gave us sandwiches made with orange cheese. I also remember when it was just the two of us playing Twenty-one he always wanted to be Michael Jordan and wanted me to be Larry Bird.

School friends were different. Everything between us was obstructed by the rules and structures of the school. We were a version of ourselves in a kind of performance for the teacher and for one another. I didn't really start having friendships that extended beyond school with any classmates until I was older, so my second white friend was also a kid I met from the neighborhood. His name was Andre, and his family lived in Key West most of the year, where he went to school with his younger brother Renny. We met on his first day of day camp at Holstein Park, where I'd been going every summer. I walked into a gymnasium and a bigger Puerto Rican kid was squeezing his neck with both hands. I ran over and told the kid to stop, which he did.

Andre and I became good friends that summer. His family bought a yellow brick house and an adjacent lot, across the park from our building, to rent out during the year and live in during hurricane season. He had a sandbox, which was the first I'd ever seen, and a ring of green and white hostas in the center of his yard, with a few mantises living in it. His mom was a painter whose work looked a lot like Keith Haring's. His dad, a barrel-chested man, always walked around with his shirt off, and when I first met him I was surprised that he smelled like armpits, because he chose not to use deodorant. I don't think I ever learned what he did.

I spent a lot of time with Andre in his yard and with his family, and for several summers I was his only real friend in the neighborhood. He was the first kid who asked me to stay for dinner, and dinner at their house was the first time I had salad with a meal, and the first time I had dinner by candlelight. There were paintings on the walls, and objects and furniture seemed to be selected and placed with careful attention to how the room would look, and how that look would make you feel. Our house wasn't a pit, but there was a conspicuous difference in how this family lived, and I remember consciously noticing these differences and enjoying being able to observe them because they were evidence of a world outside of the one I already knew.

A few summers into our friendship I introduced Andre to another friend I'd made during the year, another white kid who had moved into a newly finished condo building down the block. They hit it off, and a few weeks later I saw them hanging out together without me. The three of us continued to be friends, but things weren't the same after that. Andre and I stopped hanging out every day like we once did, and things felt chilly. A summer or two later Andre stopped coming to Chicago because his parents sold their house and adjacent lot. I watched the yellow building get gutted and rehabbed, and now there are ugly generic condos where the yard used to be. A lot of structures went up and came down in that stretch of years as the neighborhood was "revitalized." One by one, new people, mostly white, replaced neighbors until everyone I passed walking down the block was a stranger.

By the time we were priced out of the neighborhood where we'd lived since coming to the United States—the place where all my first memories were made—I was old enough to understand the nature of some of the changes that had taken place. I'd already very viscerally experienced, by witnessing gang violence, how someone's benefit could be tied directly to someone else's detriment. Anyone could learn this lesson if one walked around Bucktown long enough, but then I understood that this rule could also apply beyond observable chains of cause and effect. Andre had been my friend, and his family had been good to me, but they were a pioneering family in an already inhabited space, and despite their benevolence they were part of what would eventually drive out the people who were living there, my family included. It was the first time I really understood how some of the strong imperatives that animate social life have little to do with individual will. There were arrangements of power that relied less upon malice and more upon disregard, obliviousness, adherence to what one was accustomed, and a generally uncritical disposition toward one's own place in the world. It would have been easy to revise my view of my friendship with Andre and others like him, to believe we had never really been friends, but that simply wasn't the case. We *had* been friends and what occurred still occurred.

Caitlin walks past me toward the opening in the first iron gate. I turn toward the hills where a car snakes its way toward us, kicking up dust. She passes the first threshold and enters the zone between the double barriers. A narrow path made of sand-colored tiles cordoned off by thick steel wire leads to a corral up against the main gate—a wall of rust. At the edge of the path, the tiles disappear beneath a few scraggly weeds that grow in clusters and look like they're clutching the sand. Just beyond the narrow path there's a single dwarf tree, and leaning up against its base is a lone white cross. It makes me think about Octavio and the man who'd stopped moving as they attempted to cross, and I wonder whether word ever reached that man's family, or if now, years later, someone still waits for him to call or walk through a door.

A light-skinned lanky man walks past us to the fence. He paces back and forth, looking at his watch for a few moments. A woman on the other side approaches, pulling a toddler by the hand: a little girl in a pink cardigan, with white bows in her hair. Upon seeing them, the man crouches and presses his hand against the metal. Her fingers are small enough to poke through the spaces, so they can touch at least a little, in violation of the various posted signs that forbid any attempt at physical contact. Caitlin and I aren't close enough to understand what they're saying, but we're both immobilized watching how their bodies bend toward each other, listening to the subtle intonations of their voices. They talk for a while, their bodies curling in closer until their heads are pressed to the metal, and then, abruptly, he stands to talk with the woman. The green-and-white SUV is still there. The sunlight on the windshield prevents us from seeing inside. From where we're standing I watch the man retrieve something from his pocket. It looks like paper folded into a long thin strip, about the length of money. The woman quickly plucks it out of his hand from the other side, and then they both turn and walk away. I catch a glimpse of his eyes, which look thick and wet. He looks sallow and older than I'd originally thought, and as he marches toward his car he doesn't look back. Clouds of dust kick up in his wake as he pulls away.

Out here on this final sliver of land before the ocean, no one sees these small moments between a father, a mother, and their daughter, a girl just old enough to understand there's a real, physical barrier between her and her dad. It's often said that shedding light on events like these, making them visible, has some impact on those who learn about them. I'm sure it does, but what I'm less sure of is if the impact is great enough to radiate beyond someone's individual psychology and result in any action. The distance between being emotionally moved and actually moving is a chasm few seem to cross. I'm suspicious of those who preach awareness, or hold empathy at the center of problematics of injustice, because awareness itself has never seemed to be enough, and empathy always has, and always will have, a limited scope because of the impossibility of what it requires.

Some of the most widely held and enduring definitions of friendship rest on the idea of mutual concern. One friend cares about the welfare of the other and vice versa, but whether or not the quality of the caring ever goes beyond the realm of the emotional or psychological is much more ambiguous. There are fewer definitions that include action on the behalf of friends, perhaps because it's assumed that action follows concern, or maybe it's believed that spending time in friendship is itself nourishing for the parties involved, and that this spending time is by itself a kind of action on behalf of someone we consider a friend. But what about when action required on a friend's behalf goes beyond the everyday? There are situations when it's precisely the concern we have for others that dissolves friendships and renders us unable to act in ways our friends might really need. Serious illness, for example, a terminal diagnosis, or mental illness, can have the effect of repelling close friends. The feelings of helplessness and proximity to the anguish of someone we care deeply about can be too much to endure. In those moments it's simply easier, although not easy, to disappear.

And then there's the body of violent crime statistics

that show Americans are about as likely to be murdered by friends, relatives, and acquaintances as by strangers.

Just beyond the border, in Tijuana, there's a white lighthouse and a hotel called the Hotel Martín. A kid, maybe sixteen years old, walks his golden retriever who trots around sniffing at everything it passes. Caitlin touches my arm as we stand motionless, peering through the metal crosshatching at a quiet street.

When I moved to Iowa I lost touch with the friends I'd had in Chicago, and I was thrown into an environment I didn't immediately notice was more racially segregated than any I'd ever lived in. It took several months for me to begin to feel the almost complete absence of meaningful interaction with people of color. There were several other graduate students in my cohort who weren't white, but when we were set into the broader university community we were overwhelmed by a sea of whiteness. The graduate program I attended was supposed to be full of serious writers, people who were striving to be artists, which I mistakenly assumed meant they would be interested in engaging critically with the ways mass culture grinds people into dust, but one of the first things I noticed was that many embraced the romantic notion of the writer as a solitary being and were interested in little other than writing cleverly about their own middle-class realities. Others had adopted a shallow, non-rigorous nihilism that allowed them to be comfortably and fashionably hopeless about the course of any action. And others still, whose work verged on something meaningful, managed to file down their voices, producing "interesting" and "brave" pieces for smooth consumption, digestion, and excretion. On more than one occasion, one white friend expressed, without a trace of sarcasm, how lucky I was to be so clearly socioeconomically maligned because it put me in a great position for my writing.

. . .

The lighthouse just beyond the boundary seems like a cruel joke, a cliché symbol of finding your way home from open sea behind tons of metal that have destroyed countless homes. There's nothing ambiguous about my place here anymore, at least not officially. Officially I'm an American standing in front of a wall that's here to "protect" me from people who are not a threat to my safety or well-being. This new position is disorienting because it injures as it brings me into the fold. I'm no longer subject to the cruel and unusual punishment of being uprooted, expelled, and barred from returning for menial crimes. But it's also impossible for me not to be overwhelmed by the situation of approximately 11.5 million people, among whom friends like Octavio count themselves. Any contact with law enforcement could lead to indefinite detention and eventual expulsion, perhaps for life. Days become a walk along a dire edge, particularly for people who face added levels of structural vulnerability, like undocumented women who are often not able to report domestic abuse, sexual assault, and rape out of fear of making contact with law enforcement. Like undocumented LGBTQ populations that have been excluded from heteronormative, family-based immigration relief. Like people who have been convicted of crimes for whom almost no one advocates and who are frequently offered up as sacrificial populations for liberal reform. Since I've become a citizen, these realities that have always been very present for me have become acute. Being a brown graduate student and instructor at a primarily white institution of higher education means that in addition to the aggressive forms of racism I experience, there's a layer of mundane, casual, almost ambient racism that hangs in the halls and offices I move through. It's as though there's a piercingly high frequency going at all times that only some can hear, and when it finally knocks you off kilter, people then call you crazy. Even though my situation isn't as dire as it could be, isn't as dire as it once was, and isn't anywhere near feeling the full weight empire can bring to bear, it feels as though I'm in a kind of indefinite, never-ending battle, and the territory being ruined is me, us.

Across the political spectrum one would easily find many who know that friendship is an inane metaphor to use for the relationship between states, and I agree, but maybe the terms of this cynicism betray a deeper naïveté, one that implies an idealized form of friendship that can produce a genuine or authentic connection with another. When it happens, maybe it feels as Aristotle characterized it, one soul occupying two bodies. Two people share not only a deep and abiding concern for the other, but as the unification would suggest, a harmony of interests. We often feel this apparent union to be inherently virtuous if it's genuinely enacted, and we assume that the psychological goodness we feel radiates over the horizon of self to interpersonal relationships, and beyond into the public and political spheres. But sometimes friendship goes bad or gets stale, and sometimes it was rotten to begin with—rotten for the friends, rotten for one of them, or good for the friends and rotten for those around them. Whatever its associated feelings, it's a bounded ethical relationship. These feelings of union drive exclusion and the privileging of some over others.

In the realm of the personal, encountering strangers is still possible. I encounter people I don't properly know, and in whom I don't immediately recognize myself, people whose experience is inaccessible to understanding through my own subjectivity. I even sometimes feel as though I've encountered aspects of the foreign within the boundaries of myself. States, on the other hand, have no strangers. The existence and operations of organizations like the International Monetary Fund, the World Bank, and the World Trade Organization are evidence that the nations of the world are bound in inextricable ways. The idea that countries have control over their territory and domestic affairs to the exclusion of external powers is a fiction, a particularly brutal one for so-called developing countries who have been continually "known" by affluent states from colonialism to globalism.

Friendship *is* inane, not because we haven't been virtuous enough as a nation to achieve it, but because its metaphorical application distorts reality. It's inane to imagine the psychological constructs, motivations, impulses, and tendencies of the individual are analogous to the operations of a state.

A short man wearing a NASCAR cap and light blue jeans walks up to the boundary from the other side. His skin is dark brown like mine and he looks like he's in his late forties. He surveys the scene like maybe he's waiting for someone, but we're the only ones there. In the background a couple of cars pitter down a street we can't see, and Caitlin takes a photo of the lighthouse through the metal crosshatching. The man approaches us, nodding.

"Buenas tardes."

"Hola. Qué tal?"

He looks at both of us, and then at the fence, up and down theatrically. He says he's doing okay considering and asks us what we're doing here. Caitlin tells him we just wanted to see this thing, motioning to the wall between us. He says that down around the zona centro by Plaza de las Americas, there's a triple boundary with giant concrete blocks, and he says everything started with Pete Wilson, "that son-of-a-bitch governor who didn't even want to let the children of migrants go to school." I nod, remembering Proposition 187 from my childhood, and how it was one of the moments I came to understand my family's situation a little more accurately. The man's voice begins to tighten, and his syllables become quick when he asks how many people have died because of this goddamn fence.

"Toda esa pinche paisanada," he says, hitting his consonants hard.

He points away from the ocean and says that at the San Ysidro crossing they killed a man. I immediately recognize he's talking about Anastasio Hernandez-Rojas, who'd lived in San Diego for twenty-seven years, since he was a child, and who at the time of his killing had five children of his own. He was a taxpaying builder who was arrested and deported for shoplifting. And he had been captured trying to get back to his family. In a postmortem toxicology report he was found to have methamphetamine in his system, a fact that was widely publicized when the story broke. Two medical experts characterized the amount of methamphetamine as small, and one said it was impossible to attribute any behavior at the time of his death to the drug. Initial reports of the incident misrepresented the number of agents involved. According to a subsequent investigation by the San Diego Police Department, agents removed Anastasio's handcuffs, and he "became violent." The report says it was due to this violent behavior that agents were forced to use a Taser to subdue him. He died in the hospital. If it hadn't been for Anastasio's widow, Maria Puga, and groups of activists who supported her in her rejection of the official narrative, Anastasio's killing would have slipped quietly into oblivion—just another junked-out criminal righteously put down. But Maria and her supporters dredged up evidence. Several witnesses presented cell phone footage of the event. One video captured by Ashley Young, a woman from Seattle who was crossing back into the United States, shows a group of about twenty agents surrounding Anastasio while he's already hogtied and on the ground. It's at this point that an agent can be seen using a Taser on him. In another video agents descend violently on Anastasio as he's on the ground pleading for his life. The father and husband screams as the agents fatally injure him. Witnesses said he was offering little to no resistance.

The man moves a bit closer to the metal boundary and lowers his voice. He says he's going to tell us something he hasn't told anyone except maybe one other person. He was on a hillside a while back in a rural area around midnight when a Customs and Border Protection agent picked him up. He was cuffed and roughed up, he says. The agent kicked him a few times before loading him into his Tahoe or Suburban or whatever it was. He immediately noticed the agent was alone, and this fact scared him. He was driven to another location, a desolate clearing he didn't recognize, where the agent turned off his vehicle and got out of the car. He says that when the agent pulled him out of the backseat, he thought he was going to die. He says he was sure the agent was going to give him "ley de fuga," a well-known phrase in Mexico that refers to a kind of extrajudicial execution and cover-up that came to be known during Porfirio Díaz's dictatorship. The procedure involves agents of the state setting up scenarios in which a person is killed during an escape attempt.

The man says the agent removed his handcuffs and told him to go, but that he refused because he knew the agent was going to kill him as soon as he turned his back. He tells us he knows they would have said it was kidnappers or narcos, and that no one would have asked any questions. Add the body to the pile. Case closed. He begged and pleaded for the agent not to kill him, and eventually the officer just got back in his truck and drove away, leaving him in the wilderness to fend for himself.

CHAPTER 9

Passport
to the New West

I arrive by bus in Tucson late one afternoon and walk to a gas station where a volunteer will be picking me up. I signed up with a humanitarian aid group that leaves water in the desert for people attempting to cross the border, provides emergency medical treatment for those who may need it, and documents abuse suffered by people at various points in their journeys. By the time I make it there I'm dripping sweat because it's late July, I have a fifty pound bag strapped to my back, and the sun feels like it's a few feet away from my face. A rusted-out SUV pulls up and a young white guy with a scruffy beard rolls down his window.

"You José?"

"Yeah."

"Hop in."

Orientation for new volunteers starts a few hours later at a space the group has arranged in a small local church and school building in Tucson. A handful of young people, mostly white, sit around smoking in the courtyard for a while. We gather in a small classroom where an attorney comes in to give us some information so that we can make informed decisions in the desert. A couple of summers back, a jury of twelve convicted a volunteer of "knowingly littering"—for leaving gallons of water for people in the 110-degree desert. We're told that people drink cow tank water—stagnant pools that cows wade, urinate, and defecate in—out of necessity. A former volunteer tells us that Border Patrol and Wackenhut GS4, a contractor paid by the government to transport migrants, don't often give people water or medical attention even though they know they've been journeying through the desert for days. We're told that two volunteers, a young woman and man, were arrested, and that a grand jury charged them with two felonies: conspiracy to transport an "illegal immigrant" and transporting an "illegal immigrant." The volunteers had come upon a group of migrants who'd been traveling through the desert for four days, two days without food or water during the week that turned out to be, until then, the deadliest in Arizona history. It was over one hundred degrees Fahrenheit for forty straight days, and seventy-eight people were known to have died. The volunteers were arrested while evacuating three men to a medical facility in Tucson. They rejected a plea that would have seen all charges dropped for an admission of guilt, instead risking a sentence of up to fifteen years in prison and fines of up to five hundred thousand dollars. The proceedings dragged on for about a year and a half. Eventually the charges were dropped.

A tall older man who looks like a cowboy joins us in the classroom. He takes off his beige felt hat and wipes the white hair on his sweaty forehead. He introduces himself as John Fife, a retired Presbyterian minister and cofounder of No More Deaths (NMD). In the eighties Fife also cofounded the sanctuary movement in the United States, a network that helped Central American refugees flee US-backed death squads in El Salvador and Guatemala. He was arrested with others, and in 1986 Fife was found guilty of "conspiracy and two counts of aiding and abetting the illegal entry of Central American refugees into the US," for which he served five years of probation. He tries to talk to all the volunteer groups. He tells us what he thinks this work means and that he's glad we're here. Leaning on the wall behind him is a large map glued to a poster board. Depicting the border region south of Tucson, it's covered with hundreds of red dots, which he tells us represent the loss of human life. Almost six thousand deaths are marked on the map, and those are just the ones that have been counted.

After Fife leaves, a wilderness EMT shows us how to irrigate a wound and treat severe blisters. We learn that a moderately to severely dehydrated person needs to be given small amounts of water in intervals and that pinching someone's skin and seeing how long it takes to return to its shape is a way to gauge how dehydrated a person may be. We're told to ask everyone we encounter if they're urinating or defecating blood, because that can be a sign of a severe infection from drinking contaminated water. Each gallon of water, we're told, weighs eight and a half pounds, so it's impossible for people to carry enough. The border is eleven miles from where we'll be staying, a region of jagged mountains and arroyos that rise and fall in brutal configurations. It usually looks like a barren lunar landscape, but after monsoon season, which it is now, it's lush, and the arroyos can flood in seconds and sweep away anyone who may be walking in them to avoid detection.

Volunteers sleep in small classrooms at the church. Just before turning out the lights I see a translucent scorpion the size of a domino in the corner and crush it with one of my boots. I arrange foldout chairs in a row and manage to sleep on them. The next morning we drive sixty miles south to Arivaca with the windows down. It rained at dawn, and things are a lot more lush than I'd expected. I draw in thick air with a deep clean smell. A young woman in the car says that people think the smell is rain, but it's really rain mixing with the waxy resin of the creosote bush that gives the desert its fresh, wide-open smell after a downpour. She points out the window at brittle-looking scrub along the road. It looks unimpressive, but it may have been the bush through which God spoke to Moses in fire, and it can live for two, sometimes three years without a drop of rain. She says one of the oldest living organisms on earth is a ring of creosote that's been cloning itself for almost twelve thousand years in the Mojave.

Someone else says there's a checkpoint up ahead and that we might be asked to identify ourselves. I finger my new US passport in a Ziploc bag in my pocket. According to a 2005 report by the US Government Accountability Office, there are thirty-three "permanent" checkpoints in the Southwest border states. The number of checkpoints actually in operation is not publicly known because there are an undisclosed number of "tactical" and "temporary" ones deployed. Some news outlets report that the number is around 170. The one up ahead has "temporarily" been there for about five years, and the residents of Arivaca have to go through it whenever they need to go to a store bigger than the mercantile exchange, a small convenience store in town, or go to work, school, or anywhere other than Arivaca, really. When the Border Patrol started in 1924, it was "a handful of mounted agents patrolling desolate areas along U.S. borders." They operated within "a reasonable distance" of the boundary line, but in 1953 the federal government defined this distance as "100 air miles" from all external borders, including coasts. That means that today the more than twenty-one thousand agents of Customs and Border Protection (CBP) stomp around violating the Fourth Amendment on a land area on which about two-thirds of the US population lives. The ACLU reports that "Connecticut, Delaware, Florida, Hawaii, Maine, Massachusetts, New Hampshire, New Jersey, New York, Rhode Island and Vermont lie entirely or almost entirely within this area," and that the area contains "New York City, Los Angeles, Chicago, Houston, Philadelphia, Phoenix, San Antonio, San Diego and San Jose." I remember that a few years ago an old friend of mine was snatched off a Greyhound bus on his way home to Chicago from Cornell University.

When we pull up to the checkpoint, an agent looks inside the truck at everyone's faces. He's uninterested because we're headed toward Arivaca instead of coming from there. He asks the group if everyone's a citizen. We all say yes, and he waves us through.

Within twenty-five miles of the border, CBP agents have been given the authority to enter private property (except dwellings) without a warrant.

Arivaca is an unincorporated area of about eight hundred residents and sits twenty-three miles from Interstate 19 and eleven miles north of the border. The main street, Arivaca Road, is lined with a few small houses, some adobe structures, a small store called the Arivaca Mercantile, and La Gitana Cantina. All within about a block there are a small library, a mechanic, and a veterinarian's office. The place looks like an outpost, and as we're pulling into the Merc, a brick building painted an earthen brown with teal and peach accents, everything is quiet and slow-moving. A dried-out old man with a white beard, cowboy hat, and a six-shooter on each hip walks past us into the store, the sound of his jangling keys merging with the din of bugs buzzing in the brush. A man and woman on horseback ride down the main street, the horse's hooves clopping in an even rhythm. In the distance we can see several large vehicles barreling in our direction down Arivaca Road. Three white-and-green Border Patrol trucks, one SUV and two pickups with blacked-out windows, slow as they reach the main drag. The pickups have prisoner enclosures on the beds that look like the dog cages on the back of animal control trucks. The man and woman on horseback pull off the road and stare hard at the trucks as they pass.

We drive through Arivaca to Ruby Road. After a bit, the asphalt gives way to severe dirt terrain, so the car slows as the morning burns off and the early afternoon makes the inside of the truck feel like a dry sauna. All morning I've been thinking about that map—the red dots that looked like spilled blood covering thousands of miles, and the number of lives that have been ended on this political line. The figure comes from the Border Patrol's own tabulations, which are almost certainly low because of the unstructured, sporadic, and prohibitive ways the dead are counted. Even this low estimate means that since 1998, nearly as many people have died trying to cross the southern border into the United States as there were US soldiers killed in Iraq. Whenever I'm confronted with that figure I try to imagine them embodied, in a group, taking up space and still breathing. A room wouldn't be enough to contain the dead, nor would a warehouse—it would have to be an arena, something like a minor league baseball park packed with men, women, and children, some of whom look like they could be my aunts, uncles, cousins, nephews, parents. But most likely it would be two, three, maybe four arenas, because many bodies are never recovered and so never counted. I think about how, even if all the dead were recovered, the figure wouldn't come close to reflecting the embodied traumas of these ongoing killings. Lives aren't units to be weighed like commodities. Each one of these people was a needed member of a family. Officially there are six thousand dead—six thousand forever-open wounds. In reality the devastation is much greater than this.

Desert Camp, the center of operations for NMD, is on a parcel of rough, hilly land that belongs to Byrd Baylor, a children's book author in her late eighties who lives just a couple of miles outside of Arivaca in an adobe and stone structure without electricity. The entrance to the camp is a thick utility strap stretched between two metal fence posts. A young brown-skinned woman with a buzz cut and a black-and-red,

photorealistic tattoo of Frida Kahlo removes the strap and
lets the trucks in. There's a small clearing in the mesquite
trees and scrub with a couple of freestanding canopy structures that serve as a kitchen, office, and meeting area, flanked
by a large military surplus medical tent for anyone who may
need emergency care. We're told we can set up our tents
wherever we'd like, and I find a shady spot nestled by some
mesquite trees. Later one of the long-term volunteers asks
me why I set up my tent in Rattlesnake Ridge.

The beauty of the desert doesn't hit me until dusk. Before
that all I can feel is the sun, a searing orb too bright to look
toward, burning me through my clothes, and all I can think
is how horrific it must be to not have any way to escape it.
When we'd done a little bit of walking earlier in the day, each
step was arduous, with loose rock under every footfall shifting
my ankles violently. Nothing was flat or smooth, and mas-
sive boulders required significant climbing at points. Within
minutes it became obvious how easy it would be to succumb,
even for a young person in good health. On our drive into
camp I'd seen long stretches of jagged terrain with no more
to make shade than waist-high mesquite trees, sprawling
clusters of nopales, and ocotillo, a succulent that resembles a
cat-o'-nine-tails or a group of spindly coral fingers. It wasn't
like anything I'd imagined. The residents of Arivaca and the
Tohono O'odham people live in this desert and interact with
it knowingly and casually on a daily basis. The climate and
terrain are harsh, but they need not be deadly. It isn't expo-
sure or the natural danger of this terrain that ends people's
lives. In the Border Patrol's own articulation of their plan
to militarize the border, a document titled "Border Patrol
Strategic Plan 1994 and Beyond" the agency accepted "that
absolute sealing of the border is unrealistic." The plan instead was "to prioritize . . . efforts by geographic area." The
document includes a brief assessment of the environment of
border areas where "illegal entrants crossing through remote,

uninhabited expanses of land and sea . . . can find themselves in mortal danger." The plan specifies that cities split by the boundary line "are the areas of greatest risk for illegal entry," because these "urban areas offer accessibility to roads, rail lines, airports and bus routes to the interior of the country." The document identifies and names specific sectors that are "the locations of heaviest illegal immigration activity." They are identified as "avenues of approach" (AA) in order from most heavily trafficked areas (AA1) to least (AA12).

The plan's first phase was supposed to be accomplished in fiscal year 1994–95, and the first areas to be secured were San Diego (AA1) and El Paso (AA2). The document predicted that "as a measure of control is achieved in these corridors, some illegal traffic is expected to shift to AA4 and AA3," Arizona and South and South Central Texas respectively. This happened as predicted, and, according to the plan, in these areas the focus was on "attaining control of the urban areas first and then the rural areas." The plan has been stuck here for approximately sixteen years—in funneling people into the "most remote, uninhabited expanses of land" through the harshest avenues of approach.

At dusk a meeting is called, and as I'm waiting on a folding chair around an extinguished campfire for the rest of the group to gather, I feel utterly overwhelmed by the desert. I'd expected to see something barren, reflective of death and dying, but everything is fecund, verdant—teeming. Just beside me, shooting up through the hard earth, are a few long stalks punctuated at their ends by bursts of purple and yellow flowers smaller than an infant's pinky nail. Beyond the edge of the clearing the brush is so thick it seems impossible to walk through without a machete to clear a path. In the middle distance, perhaps a thousand yards from the edge of camp, rise two hills in black silhouette against an indigo, cerulean, and fuchsia sky. This is the first time I see the group together—a motley collection, mostly white women, two women of Mexican lineage, me, and three or four white men. One of the young white women facilitates the meeting. Mostly it's about how the water drops are done and protocols for situations we may encounter. She finishes by saying it'll be important for us to stay in larger groups this week because a PBS program that used NMD footage aired last night.

Just over two months ago, on the morning of May 14, a camera placed by volunteers captured three agents in bulky green gear walking along a trail at the edge of a cliff. There are six plastic gallons of water visible. The middle agent, who appears to be a blonde white woman, kicks the gallons off the ledge one by one. Some explode when her boot meets them, their tops bursting off, and some survive the initial kick only to tear open on the jagged rocks below. The agent in front, also white, stops to watch and smile. The third agent's face is obscured by his movements.

The kind of cruelty captured on the video isn't an anomaly. NMD conducted a study in which they found that denial of food and water is common, even when migrants are in custody for multiple days and even though most people taken into custody are already experiencing some form of dehydration. Ten percent of interviewees, including teens and children, reported physical abuse, and "of the 433 incidents in which emergency medical treatment or medications were needed, Border Patrol provided access to care in only 59 cases." One interviewee, a woman who said she had lived in the United States for seventeen years with three children, said agents had made her strip naked. "Then they took her clothes and touched her breasts." A man from Chiapas reported being kicked to the ground while being apprehended and having a cactus needle lodged in his eye. He was held in custody for forty-eight hours and did not receive medical attention before being repatriated. One female interviewee reported seeing a pregnant woman with a fever requesting to go to the hospital. The guards didn't believe she was pregnant, and she suffered a miscarriage. A sixteen-year-old boy from Guatemala reported being struck in the back of the head with a flashlight and being held in custody for three days, during which time he only received a packet of cookies and one juice box each day. Several men recounted being hit with the butt of a gun during apprehension. One man reported that migra corridos, macabre songs about death and killing in the desert, were played twenty-four hours a day at extreme volumes, and that every two hours shouting guards would rush their cells and make them line up for inspection. The report concluded:

> It is clear that instances of mistreatment and abuse in Border Patrol custody are not aberrational. Rather, they reflect common practice for an agency that is part of the largest federal law enforcement body in the country. Many of them plainly meet the definition of torture under international law.

That night it was impossible for me to fall asleep. I lay awake looking up at the camouflage fabric of the single-person tent I'd borrowed, the moon illuminating the lighter patches. I analyzed every snap of mesquite branch and crackling in the brush, having no firm walls to give me a false sense of security. Before coming to the desert I'd been traveling in California, staying with friends and friends of friends, basically anyone who would let me sleep on their couch or floor. In one of those coincidences that are so eerily fitting people usually imbue them with significance that isn't there, I'd ended up staying in the home of a former Army Ranger sniper, who was currently interning at the Department of Homeland Security and hoping to become an Immigration and Customs Enforcement agent. I learned this information my first evening in his home when we were making small talk, and I tried not to react visibly when he told me. There was no significance to our meeting. He lived near the border, was ex-military, and needed a better job than the security gig he currently had. He set me up in his son's bedroom, while the kid stayed with his mother. He let me borrow a tent and gave me an old MRE. On one of the walls of his son's bedroom hung a green felt banner with the famous Hemingway quote: "There is no hunting like the hunting of man, and those who have hunted armed men long enough and liked it, never really care for anything else thereafter."

Hours pass in the liminal space between sleep and waking. My body goes numb and I glide just below the surface of sleep, but really I'm just waiting. At one point I think I hear sounds outside the tent, and these sounds merge into the dream I'm having before they become crisp enough to bring me back to waking consciousness. Then a few moments pass before I regain the ability to move. I open my eyes and lie perfectly still, overtaken by fear. It takes a few blinks before I remember where I am, why I'm staring up at patches of green-and-black camouflage fabric. I'm still afraid, but the knowledge that there might be someone injured or dying in the darkness overwhelms my fear. I slowly unzip a corner of the tent to peek toward the sounds. Another volunteer, whose tent is thirty feet from mine, is doing the same. It sounds like someone or something is moving in the brush just beyond the clearing of camp. We listen for several minutes, trying to get a sense of what's making the noise. Earlier in the day, I'd noticed that sounds don't carry in the desert. It's as if there's a moving wall between you and everything else, so you can only hear what's in the immediate vicinity. Now it sounds like twigs and dry plant material shifting underfoot. Whenever there's a loud snap it's followed by several minutes of silence.

Each moment of this waiting seems to move thickly, as if it's clotted and obstructing its own passage. When I decide I need to get out of my tent, I don't have faith that nothing will happen to me, but I make a calculation and determine that I'm going. I put on my headlamp but don't turn it on and feel my way toward a long-term volunteer's tent to wake her. She's already listening to the sounds. The other volunteer who also heard the sounds joins us, and we decide we'll light a campfire, sit by it, and call out periodically. We can't approach the sound too closely because we might cause someone to flee, or a group to scatter. She says people won't reveal themselves until they know we're friendly. We stumble toward the edge of camp in darkness, looking out into a valley of black shapes edged in moonlight. *Somos amigos*, we're friends. *Por favor no tengan miedo*, please don't be afraid. *Tenemos agua y comida*, we have water and food. *Tenemos gente que los puede curar si necesitan atención médica*, we have people who can help if you need medical attention. *No somos la patrulla fronteriza*, we are not Border Patrol.

We sit by the fire and call out every few minutes. Slowly other volunteers come and join us. One brings his guitar and plucks a few chords while we sit and wait in the small circle of flickering orange light. It's surprising how cold it gets at night, and everything is covered in fat drops of dew. I watch one small droplet merge with another and then another on the slick metal surface of a bucket until it becomes so fat it falls to the sand. We call out in intervals for about an hour until we hear several vehicles barreling down the only road around camp toward a hill in the distance. A dozen beams of light converge on a hillside, and we hear vehicle doors open and slam, and then screaming and commands, some in English. Several smaller beams appear, cutting into the distance while trembling—flashlights in the hands of running Border Patrol agents—and we can actually hear the sound of bodies colliding. One of the beams tumbles down a hill. There are more screams, muffled, as though the screamer's mouth is pressed against a body or the ground, and then someone yells "Viva México, hijos de su puta madre!"

Things go quiet for a while. People are loaded into vehicles and driven away, and then everything is dark again, no more lights on the hillside. Those who were captured may have been the people we heard in the brush, or the people in the brush may have been others separated from the rest of the group. One of the long-term volunteers tells us sometimes people get away, that they might be hiding in the area, and that if their guide was arrested, tomorrow they'll be much more likely to walk without direction until they die. She goes to a storage container the size of a tool shed, full of food and water, unlocks it, and turns a sign welcoming anyone to take what they need. We put out a dozen gallons of water at the entrance to camp, and we place another dozen in a wash that runs behind the area where my tent is. The volunteer tells us that most of the individuals they've encountered in the last few years have been trying to get back to their families, families from whom they were torn after living in the United States together for years, sometimes decades. The overall number of people attempting to migrate has nearly come to a standstill because of the economic downturn, but the number of people dying in the desert has remained about the same. This means when people decide they need to do this, when they say good-bye to their friends and loved ones and set off, they're much more likely to be saying their final good-byes. Since the recovery and identification of remains is far from a certainty for people who die in the desert, they may simply disappear. Their families stop hearing from them, and rather than ever reaching a point of finality, the trauma remains ambiguous, open, and ongoing.

We park the truck on a ridge lined with ocotillos and a couple of spherical sotols, with their long alien-like flowers jutting seven feet into the air. A paloverde punctuates the distance with its chartreuse leaves and green trunk that performs photosynthesis. The three of us set out on foot, and we're guided by a handheld GPS. I'd been given a laminated topographical map of the area to practice finding our location by physical landmark, but after a few minutes I completely lose orientation. I turn the map again and again, looking out toward endless hills, searching without success for something in the landscape to anchor me onto the lines of the map. I put it in my pocket. A few minutes later we're hiking in silence on the bed of a broad wash with cragged walls like a reef. I hadn't anticipated long periods of silence or the strange acoustic quality in the air that makes this endless space sound and feel at times like being in a diving bell. I'd assumed the extremity of the conditions would keep my attention squarely in the work my body was exerting, but as rocks shifted under my feet, I think about the people out here crossing and about my own relation to this place. Simply being out here isn't dangerous, at least not inherently so. The blue passport in my pocket means the likelihood of me dying out here is close to zero. It means what I'm doing is closer to a workout or a leisure activity than a struggle to remain alive. I think about how, in the past, I've rejected claims put upon me by other Mexicans, wanting to assert myself as an individual rather than a member of a group, but for some time now those feelings have shifted, and I've felt a solidarity with others who are under attack.

After five minutes of walking, the woman in front pitches to the right, stumbles, and finally lands hard on the ground, smashing one of the gallons of water she'd been carrying. Her ankle immediately swells, so we collectively decide we'll help her back to the truck, and then the other volunteer and I will make the drop. After we drop her off and head back out, though, we get lost, despite having the GPS telling us where to go. It's noon, and the sun is directly overhead. My skin begins to throb, and it becomes imperative that I cover my head. I soak a bandana with some of my drinking water and drape it so that it covers the top of my head and nape. It's dry in less than five minutes. It takes us a little under an hour to move forward one mile to the drop, and as we're approaching I spot a flash of movement to the left. When I turn I think I see two figures bound away and disappear between mesquite trees, but I don't at all know what I've seen. My impression is that they were big, about the size of a person or large animal, and that there were two, but even that's unclear. I begin calling out, saying we have water and food, and that we're from the church, we're not BP, we're friends. We continue walking and make the drop, and I continue calling out for a long time as we make our way back toward the vehicle, but there's no response.

In this border region, the horizon between natural violence and state violence has been collapsed. The arid climate, the flash floods, the diamondbacks, the mountain impasses, the distance, and the heat of the sun have all been weaponized. People's apathy, disregard, and xenophobia have been weaponized. The situation in which death occurs has been manufactured as such. This is murder without a murderer, administered through bureaucracy and policy planning, murder with the most refined form of impunity, where not only is no one held responsible for the killing of an individual, but no one *can* be held responsible for the individuals who succumb to the journey. The responsibility of having set off into the desert is put solely on the migrants themselves.

A few days later the reality of being in a militarized zone becomes impossible to ignore. Another humanitarian aid group calls to let us know that after a water drop they found a sign on one of their vehicles saying they were being watched. It was signed "Arizona Border Recon," the name of a vigilante group that patrols the border and is listed as a "nativist extremist group" by the Southern Poverty Law Center. I knew before coming out here that encountering militia or armed vigilante groups was a possibility, especially considering many groups operate in the area with the tacit consent of some local authorities. They're regularly allowed to make citizen's arrests, go on armed patrols wearing colors, gear, and identifying patches with logos and names that resemble law enforcement uniforms, and hold people under false pretenses until they can be handed over to Border Patrol. When we take to the trails I try to focus on how it's statistically unlikely for someone in Arizona to be killed or maimed by a member of one of these groups, but I can't help feeling that my odds are different as a brown person on the border. A little over two months before I arrived in the desert, I'd read about how Jason Todd Ready, a neo-Nazi, former candidate for state legislature, and founder of two armed border vigilante groups (Minutemen Civil Defense Corps and the US Border Guard), entered the home he shared with his girlfriend, Lisa Mederos, and fatally shot her, her twenty-three-year-old daughter Amber, Amber's fiancée Jim, and Lisa's fifteen-month-old daughter Lilly, before killing himself. Authorities retrieved a small arsenal, including six grenades from the home. At the time of his death, Ready was being investigated by the FBI for domestic terrorism charges in connection with migrants who had been found shot dead near the border in southern Arizona.

A year and a half before that, one of Ready's associates, Jeffrey Harbin, was arrested on a public highway in Arizona while in possession of an explosive device that contained ball bearings that upon detonation would tear into more human flesh, break more bones, and destroy more body parts than an explosion alone could. In May 2009, Shawna Forde, the founder of a group called Minutemen American Defense, planned and executed a home invasion in Arivaca with two accomplices. The target was Raul Flores, a man Forde and her associates believed was a drug smuggler with large amounts of drugs and money in his home. Their plan was to impersonate Border Patrol agents and rob smugglers in order to fund their operations on the border. When they entered the Flores home, they found no money or drugs but shot and killed Raul and his nine-year-old daughter anyway.

It would be easy to dismiss these events as outliers and the individuals who carried them out as extremist lunatics, but many enjoyed camaraderie and privileged positions at speaking events attended by state officials and members of local governments. Ready even ran for a Mesa City Council seat in 2006 and was called a "true patriot" by former Arizona state senator Russell Pearce. Mainstream elected officials like Pearce, Jan Brewer (governor of Arizona from 2009 to 2015), and Joe Arpaio (sheriff of Arizona's Maricopa County) made careers out of appealing to white supremacists, nativists, hate groups, and their sympathizers, counting them among their voters and donors. They accrued political capital from remaining ambiguous about people like Ready, their racist rhetoric, and the climate of violent xenophobia these individuals have fomented. Their policy initiatives have often been supported by those who identify as white supremacists and, more broadly, by a sizable population of Arizonans who don't. This kind of crossover between hate groups and the general voters of Arizona is disturbing, but even more disturbing is that liberal policy makers' calls for a national security paradigm are not so different from a white supremacist wish list. The grim reality is that the manipulation of migrant flows into the deadliest parts of the Sonoran Desert has been a bipartisan affair. This national policy, and how we choose to think of and delineate our political community, has killed and continues to kill more people than Ready, Forde, or any other armed terrorist ever could.

Five of us are in a pickup truck when suddenly there's a violent gust of wind and a rushing staccato *thuk thuk thuk thuk* sound rushing toward us. An all-black helicopter with blacked-out windows and no markings rips across the landscape fifty feet in front of the truck. It's flying so low it's framed in the windshield. The driver slams on the brakes, and the helicopter tips forward, kicking up a huge cloud of dust. When it dissipates, the helicopter is gone. After the *thuk thuk thuk thuk* is in the distance and then gone completely, the driver says that BP helicopters are green and white, and that we may have activated one of the seismic sensors buried in undisclosed locations throughout the desert. "Then why the fuck was this one black?" asks someone in the backseat. The truck has started rolling again, and before anyone has time to posit a theory about the color of the chopper, a BP SUV pops over a hill and cuts down fast in front of our truck, blocking our path and almost causing a head-on collision. Several other SUVs and three men on ATVs wearing dark helmets, clad in body armor, and carrying assault rifles surround us. All of them scream commands at the same time so we can't understand any of their words. After a few tense moments, when they've calmed down a bit and verified all of our identities and immigration statuses, they still remain openly hostile, and a few of the agents duck and peer into the backseat of the car, locking onto my brown face. It all happens too fast for me to become scared in the moment, but later, after we're back at camp, I wonder how much danger we were actually in. A study conducted by the Police Executive Research Forum examined cases when BP officers discharged their firearms. One scenario they examined was agents shooting into vehicles, and they found that "most reviewed cases involved non-violent suspects who posed no threat other than a moving vehicle." The study found that, in many cases, agents "intentionally put themselves into the exit path of the vehicle, thereby exposing themselves to additional risk and creating justification for the use of deadly force." According to the report, "The cases suggest that some of the shots at suspect vehicles are taken out of frustration." It concludes, "As with vehicle shootings, some cases suggest that frustration is a factor motivating agents to shoot."

That evening as the sun disappears behind a hill I try to trap a black widow that's made its home in a screw hole at the table where volunteers eat meals. A black cat named Luther who hangs around camp watches me while lying on his side, flicking his tail. Some people are in their tents, and others are sitting and talking quietly by the campfire. I go to join them because the evening conversations have been illuminating. Most of the other volunteers are white, and I notice I feel close to them in a way that's impersonal but intimate. I don't know very much about their biographies—we're just leaving the realm of being strangers to each other—yet I felt that these white people care for me, and others like me, in ways many of my white friends at home don't. Before coming to camp I'd assumed most people would have very similar conceptions of what's happening out here and what it means more broadly, but after several nights of long conversations the only overlap everyone seemed to share was the political primacy of human life—the conviction that any and all politics should emerge from this primacy. I noticed a lot of the residents of Arivaca left gallons of water on their doorsteps and on their property, and one afternoon in La Gitana, the only bar in town, I talked to an old rancher who after a long conversation said "I'm a Republican. I don't give a damn what these people are doing out here—they shouldn't be dying."

I follow Luther over to a shrine in a clearing. I'd been avoiding it since I got here, but Luther walked by me pressing his body on the front of my calf and I was compelled to follow him. The shrine is a pile of sun-bleached objects found in the desert. Placed next to a weathered log are a calling card with a shampoo ad on the front in which a brunette runs her fingers through her hair, an empty tan backpack, a pink wallet with a silkscreened cartoon princess, a small plaster statue of praying hands with a few fingers cracked off, a plastic pocket-sized Virgen de Guadalupe, a dirty and tattered Mexican flag, a photograph or drawing in a silver frame so bleached it looks like a human figure made of light, and a plaster statue of a kneeling, praying angel. At the very front of the pile is a stone slab with a candle in the center and a few rosaries, pesos, quetzales, and quarters surrounding it. A red-and-white Santería necklace is coiled around the candle. Its small glass beads are mostly white, meaning it represents Obatalá the father, creator of human bodies, of the city of Ife, and the owner of all heads. As our sculptor, he's tasked with our protection and acts as a guardian for those otherwise without one.

Luther rubs his slender black body on my leg again before he stops directly in front of the shrine. It's uncanny, but he sits there for a while, seemingly considering the objects, quietly observing. On the trail earlier we'd come upon a small green backpack. It had been chilling to see an abandoned object on the remote trail where we were, surrounded by unforgiving hills for miles and miles. I wondered under what circumstances it was left behind, but quickly forced myself to stop thinking. One of the other volunteers said we needed to look inside for anything that might identify the person. I took a step toward it, but the volunteer grabbed my shoulder and pulled me back.

"With a stick," she said.

It was empty, except for a few food wrappers and a used rehydration packet that NMD and other groups leave at water drops. Weeks later, when I get back home, I'll find out that this month, July 2012, was the hottest month in more than 117 years on record, in more than 1,400 months. Seeing the electrolyte packet spent and discarded unsettled me. It brought two opposed realities together: the extreme value of the act of placing water in the desert but also its extreme limitation. I bend down to join Luther, looking at the individual objects that comprise the shrine; they had all been touched, carried, and imbued with some special meaning by those who gave them, and those who kept them. One dead man who was found and brought to the Pima County Medical Examiner's Office carried a dead hummingbird carefully wrapped in cloth in his pocket. Whatever the specific meaning of each individual object, it seems appropriate that they are kept in a shrine because they had always acted as prayers: repositories for hopes, fears, desires, and necessities too big to bear alone.

That night I decide to sleep outside. I set up a cot from the medical tent next to the food storage container, unlock it, and turn the sign encouraging people to take whatever they need. The moon is full behind a layer of glowing white clouds, and every once in a while it peeks through a gap, creating a halo that makes it look like a giant eye. Somehow, it's dark and at the same time the whole sky glows, making the tops of the black trucks shine. When I first got to the desert I wouldn't have slept outside, but now I feel strangely at ease, knowing that my tent—a few poles and a thin layer of fabric—doesn't provide protection from anything anyway except maybe rain. As I start to fall asleep, something in my peripheral vision catches my attention. I turn slowly toward it and see a few thick hairs on several finger-like legs climbing up my shoulder. It takes a few steps onto my chest, and I see the fat, bulbous body of a tarantula. I remain perfectly still. It takes a few more steps onto my torso and rests for a long while near the center of my chest. My impulse is to swat it away, and it takes every ounce of will to sit perfectly still and let it finish its climb all the way across my body, back down a cot leg, and into the brush.

I wake up shortly after the sun rises when the insides of my eyelids glow red because there's nothing to obstruct its rays. I'm covered in the moisture that accumulated and soaked into the various layers I wore to sleep, so I take off my outer shirt and wring it into Luther's water bowl, which is just next to my cot. My eyes are filmy, and the lids feel sticky as I blink and scan camp. No one else is up yet. I notice the door to the food storage container is slightly ajar, which it shouldn't be. Last night I opened the padlock but left it in the door so animals wouldn't get in. The dirt around me is disturbed, and when I blink a few more times, clearing my vision, I see that it's covered in hundreds of shoeprints. I pop up and yell for others to wake. I check the storage container, and a few large bags full of food and rehydration kits are gone. About two dozen packets of new socks have also been taken. From under the white tarp where donated clothes are kept, a volunteer yells that some shoes, pants, and shirts are also gone. Someone else yells from the kitchen tarp that the refrigerator is nearly empty. There are footprints all around my cot, some less than a foot away from where I slept.

Places like Arivaca, and other southwestern border regions, are often thought of and depicted as lawless, dangerous vestiges of the old West. Border Patrol agents are thus valorized as heroic law enforcers, but since being out here I've felt most in danger when the Border Patrol shows up. Since 2003, thirty-three CBP agents are listed as having "died in the line of duty." Of the thirty-three, only three were murdered. Of the others, one was killed by friendly fire. Fifteen died in car accidents, two when agents' vehicles hit large animals in the road. Four drowned. Three hearts gave out. Three aircraft crashed. Four agents collapsed. The *Washington Post* reported that during a two-year period between 2008 and 2010 fifteen agents committed suicide, meaning that during that same period more agents died by their own hand than in all other ways combined.

On one of my last days in the desert a group of us drives toward a drop location deep in the Buenos Aires National Wildlife Refuge. Almost two weeks at camp has been a dose of concentrated something, but I'm not sure what. Later,

when I get back to my life, the effects of being out here really start to become apparent. When a news helicopter flies
overhead in Tucson I wince, and for a long time I can't look
white people in the eye without feeling a pinprick of rage I
have to work hard to contain. I can't concentrate on anything
because the August sun on my skin and the record-breaking
heat in which I move keep me constantly thinking about
how, *now, right now*, there are people walking in the desert.
I spend the rest of the summer drinking heavily, compul-
sively, with the intended purpose of blacking out. And when
this feeling of catastrophic urgency starts to fade, I feel a
paralyzing guilt. In the backseat of the pickup between two
volunteers I'm trying to formulate in language why I've come
out here, not as an explanation for them, just for me, inside
my head, but there isn't a singular reason I can pin down. It's
more like an accumulation of intensity that has reached a
point of saturation and needed to be spent, a sense of obliga-
tion, and a rage.

Up ahead, about fifty feet beyond the windshield, I see a
gray ironwood tree full of fat black buzzards. One of them
glides to the ground to a dark mound and begins tearing. I
point at it without being able to say a word, and the others
in the back with me gasp and then look in silence. I tap the
driver on the shoulder, lean forward, and point.

"I see it," she says.

A few of the other buzzards glide down and join the first
one. The person to my right clenches my forearm, and I feel
like there's something pushing down on my diaphragm. Music I hadn't known was playing is turned off. The sound of
my own breathing fills the space. It becomes shallow and
spastic, picks up speed as the truck slows down. The buzzards' fat bodies covered in shiny black feathers obstruct the
mound, their horrible black heads darting down and then
jutting up when the flesh gives way. The car stops, and the
driver honks the horn. They all take off in a black cloud, and

the mound becomes visible. It's a blue-black pile from which a large round ribcage protrudes.

"It's too big. It's too big!" says the driver, out of breath. "It's a cow! It's a fucking cow!"

I let go of the headrest I was clutching, and for the rest of the drive no one says a word.

When we get to the drop we find gallons of water with the tops slashed off and cans of beans with the pull-tabs removed. There's a yellow plastic rosary hanging from the branch of the tree under which the empty gallons are strewn. We collect them and replace them with full ones.

On our way back, on a dirt road not far from camp, we see six men struggling to remain upright and moving forward. When they hear the truck, four of them let themselves fall to the ground, and the other two throw their arms up to flag us down. As we approach, our driver, a tall white woman volunteer, tells us she has medical training and thinks a Spanish speaker should stay with her. She says the truck should be driven to camp and not come back for at least an hour. She explains that since they're on a main road approaching town, BP has probably already been alerted of their presence. We'll want to treat the men as quickly and as best we can before agents arrive. So many people go through the entire process of apprehension and repatriation without receiving medical attention, being given any or enough water, or being fed much (if at all), and almost no one is informed of rights. She also explains that we want to stay and observe the apprehension because our presence might deter a beating or other forms of abuse, at least during these moments.

The two of us get out of the truck with a backpack full of emergency medical supplies, four gallons of water each, and a few packs of food. The truck takes off down the road. Two of the men, the two still standing, are unmistakably brothers, in their late twenties or early thirties.

"Hola, muchachos, somos amigos. Por qué no nos senta-
mos aquí en la sombra?" I say.

"Gracias, gracias."

They all nod, and we help the ones who are already sitting to stand back up, which looks painful for all of them but
especially agonizing to one who pulls hard on my hand as he
stands without bending his left leg.

"Me jodí la pierna, carnal."

Their eyes look the kind of tired no amount of sleep can
fix. They're all wearing tattered blue jeans and their shoes
are curled upward from walking countless miles on uneven
terrain. We help them all sit in a small clearing near a tree
that provides a few slivers of shade. I tell them we're friends,
friends with a humanitarian aid group, as we crack open a
gallon of water for each of them and advise them to drink
it slowly or they won't be able to keep it down. One of the
brothers says they want to turn themselves in to Border Patrol—*no more, no more, we want to go home.* The other volunteer begins explaining in English what the process of turning
themselves in will be like, that they'll be offered voluntary
departure papers to sign, and that they'll tell them if they
sign them they won't be charged with a crime. We explain
that a first crossing attempt isn't a felony and that they have
the right to a trial if they want to have one. We give all of
them cards with a phone number for pro bono legal aid in
Tucson and several other numbers, including that of Grupo
Beta, a group funded by the Mexican government that offers
assistance and shelter to newly repatriated migrants. I tell
them they might be transported laterally along the border
and repatriated hundreds of miles from where they crossed,
but that calling Grupo Beta will at least provide them with
information about whatever sector they find themselves in,
and that they'll pay half the price of a bus ticket back home.
I remind them they have a right to demand a phone call once

they're back at the station, and that agents might lie and tell them they don't have this right when in fact they do.

One of the brothers has been smiling at me as I speak, and when I pause he asks me if I'm from Puebla. I smile and tell him I'm from Veracruz, recognizing that he asked because we both have the flat accent of central Mexico, specifically the accent that Poblanos have. Jarochos, people from Veracruz, usually speak a bit more emphatically, while Poblanos have a slower, rounder cadence. I tell him my mother is from Puebla, but since I wasn't raised in Veracruz, and since my mother was the one whose Spanish I modeled because my old man was always working, I spoke Spanish like a Poblano without ever having lived in Puebla. The group cracks up.

"Cabrón," says one of them, slapping the ground laughing.

One of the brothers asks the other if he's hallucinating, seeing another paisa all the way out here, laughing and tugging on his brother's shirtsleeve.

We ask them how their feet are as we begin untying their shoes. The other volunteer retrieves blister kits from the backpack and begins washing one of the men's feet. A thick yellow bubble nearly covers the entire sole of his right foot. He winces as she lances it with a sterile needle and begins pressing the liquid out slowly. I give each of them a new pair of socks, which they take as if I were handing them the most precious gift. I ask the man who couldn't bend his leg earlier if I can see his knee. His jeans are already torn, but he tears the hole a bit more and shows me his kneecap, which is the size and shape of a baseball. I give him an icepack and aspirin and tell him he has the right to receive medical attention, that his kneecap might be fractured, and that he can demand to see a doctor. The other volunteer asks me to ask the group if they're sure they want to call BP, and they all nod.

"Sí. Ya. Ya no más, cabrón."

She calls while I ask the two who look like brothers who's older. They both smile, and one raises his hand slightly.

"Yo."

Even though his face is pained and his eyes are half closed, his smile is genuine, and I can tell that, at least in these moments, he and the others feel somewhat at ease. They made the trek through a *pollero*, which most people now have to do, so this is probably the first time in many days—maybe weeks—that they're dealing with someone who isn't harsh and from whom they don't feel imminent danger. The other volunteer is done wrapping the man's foot. He thanks her, and she says you're welcome in heavily accented Spanish. They share a smile.

She shuffles over to another man with a blister that runs along the outside arch of his foot from heel to toe. I ask the group if any of them are urinating or defecating blood. A few of them look at each other, but no one immediately answers. I explain that if they drank contaminated water they may have a severe infection and that they probably won't be given medication in custody. Two of the men signal with their hands. I remind them we're not doctors but that my partner is a certified wilderness EMT. She asks if they're allergic to any medication, and I translate. She gives them a strong single-dose antibiotic.

A few of them have ripped open Clif Bars and crackers and are struggling to swallow what they've chewed. One man says they've been walking for four days and that the night before last they went to sleep, and when they woke up, the rest of the group, including their guide, was gone. They had run out of water the following morning. Another man asks me how long I've lived "on this side" and how my family got here. I tell him as briefly as I can, and when I finish, the younger brother from Puebla asks what my mother's maiden name is. I tell him, and I also tell him *her* mother's maiden name and my grandfather's name. He says he knows some people with the last name Flores, who live near his family. I brush it off, until he says the grandfather is tall, abnormally so, and very dark with light-colored eyes and white hair, so they sometimes call him El Puro because he looks like a lit cigar. I remember Yoli showing me a photo of her father as a young man standing with five of his brothers, a couple of them towering over the others, and her telling me some of my great uncles were over six feet tall. The photo was sepia, and all of them were a deep brown with shiny foreheads, slicked back hair, and strangely light eyes.

For a moment it feels like I'm among family.

We all hear a car in the distance. Some of the men who'd been lying down sit up. The other volunteer is finishing wrapping one of their feet. I tell them to put the card we gave them in their pockets and to remember they're entitled to a phone call. Their faces change, tighten, and the man with the knot on his knee extends his hand to the other volunteer.

"Gracias, muchacha," he says.

"De nada," she answers, shaking his hand.

Both brothers look at me, their faces communicating more than they ever could with words: the arbitrariness of why I'm helping them rather than the other way around; the meaninglessness of it; how this absence of meaning may not make the brutality worse but somehow casts it in an even harsher light; and some relief because they think it's over, and the worst of it might be, but it might not. We shake hands. One of them pats me on the chest with his open palm after he lets go of my hand.

"Gracias, hermano."

The green-and-white SUV skids to a halt on the dirt road. We hear a car door open and close. We walk toward the road and I round a bush into visibility. When I do, the agent, a tall blond white man with a flattop, takes a step back, extending one hand while the other hand reaches back toward his belt.

"What the hell!" he yells.

"Hi, hi, hi," I say, putting my hands out with my palms open and turned upward. "We're volunteers, we're with the church."

"Get down! Sit down! On the ground!" He's yelling and signaling violently with his outstretched hand, the other one still back, hovering above his gun. We sit down.

"You—come over here," he says, pointing at the other volunteer.

She stands up slowly and walks toward him. They go to the back of the vehicle, and from where I'm sitting I can see the agent looking and signaling in my direction, obviously asking questions about me. After a minute or so they walk back, he stares at me with his eyebrows furrowed, looking perhaps a little confused. My beard was already three weeks long before I arrived in the desert, so now it's a little over an inch and unruly. It curls upward on one side along my jaw line with a few ringlets by my ears and none of it stays matted down. I'm wearing expensive cargo pants my dad insisted on buying at an outdoor store before I came out, and screen-printed on my T-shirt is a photo of an old-timey man panning for gold, with a caption that reads: "I'm not a gold digger, I'm a panhandler."

"You—come here." He signals for me to stand and follow.

The three of us walk to the group of men. When we get there, the agent radios for another vehicle. He tells us to sit, and he approaches the men who are all still in a half moon under the shade of a scraggly tree. He gets uncomfortably close, towering over them as he yells, "Yo, Steven. Okay? Bway-no? Okay. Ha ha ha." A few of the men strain to smile and nod as he says this, and a few of the others just look toward the ground.

"See, I'm nice. I'm a nice guy. Okay? Bway-no?"

He stands over me so that I have to crane my neck back at an extreme angle, looking almost directly up. He lowers his volume and changes his tone dramatically, like he's trying to make small talk.

"So, you from around here?" he asks me, ignoring the other volunteer.

"No, I live in the Midwest."

"Oh, yeah? Where? I have some family out there."

"Iowa."

I don't want to flat out refuse to answer his questions because I don't want to anger him so that he might take his frustration out on the men, or someone else he encounters after we've split.

"Oh, wow. Ha! So are you *from* Iowa?"

"I lived in Illinois before that."

"So, is English your, uh, fir—uh, first language?"

"I speak mostly English now, yes."

A voice comes over his radio, and he steps back to the vehicle for a moment. We tell the men to keep drinking water and eating. When he comes back he points at me and tells me to translate what he's going to say. He asks the men a few questions through me and then says, "Well, if you'd only done things the right way, I wouldn't have to slap these cuffs on you. I don't know why so many people can't just follow the law. It's the law. Lah-*lay*. Lah-*lay*." Instead of translating what he's just said, I remind the men they don't have to sign voluntary departure papers if they think they may qualify for some kind of immigration relief, and that someone at the number on the card can help determine if they might qualify.

"Okay, well, you two better take off now," he says, signaling to me and the other volunteer. "I'm nice, as you can see, but my partner who's on his way now is crazy. *I* don't care if you're here, but he's crazy. You better get outta here."

The other volunteer tells him we're waiting for our ride and they should be arriving any minute. He shakes his head at us.

"Don't say I didn't warn you."

He approaches the men and begins taking their back-
packs and bags of food, tossing them into a pile. He tells
them to put down the gallons of water and starts riffling
through the bags.

"Back up, then. Go over there, on the other side," he
points across the road where he wants us to move. The other
volunteer starts to pick up our supplies, putting them in the
medical pack one by one. She looks me in the eye as she's
doing it, communicating that I should also start picking up
garbage and supplies as slowly as possible, one by one, so we
can remain within eyesight longer.

Another BP vehicle arrives, this one a pickup with a cage
on the bed. The first agent approaches it. A man who looks
like a caricature of police—a close-cropped haircut, aviators,
and a push-broom mustache—gets out of the car. He too juts
back when he sees me.

"What the fuck! Who the fuck is *that*?" he says to the
first agent, pointing at me.

The first agent grabs him by the shoulder, turning him
away from us. They whisper to each other for a minute, and
then the newly arrived agent goes to the men. The first agent
stands above us.

"Go to the other side. Now. *Now!*"

We stand in the middle of the road where we can still see
the men. The agents tell them to stand. They struggle to get
up. The agents grab the gallons of water and start dumping
them out.

"Come on, man," I say.

Both of them look at us, and then at each other.

"Please let them take some water," says the other volunteer calmly.

"No, no, no. We can't. We don't know what's in these."

"We have sealed ones. Please. They're dehydrated," says
the other volunteer.

They look at each other again.

"Okay, give me the sealed ones. We'll take them in the truck with us."

"Can't they take them in the back with them? Please."

"No."

The agents make the men turn toward the tree, interlock their fingers on the backs of their heads, and spread their legs. They begin manhandling and patting them down one by one. It becomes apparent that what I'm witnessing is an act of empire-building. Here, in this zone, and on these bodies, America defines itself by what it's not. Each rejection, each death in the desert, is a re-articulation of our foundational violence. This is America. Each passage and inscription of a human being as "illegal" is a reiteration. We are in the zone where justice reaches its vanishing point, sheds its veneer, and reveals itself fully as punishment.

The agents have the men at the back of the pickup. The one with the mustache unlocks the cage and opens the door. The agent shoves the younger brother forward, and the young man braces himself on the frame and looks over to us.

"Adiós, carnales."

Each man says good-bye before they're shoved in. One of them pokes his fingers through small slots in a metal grate at the very back of the cage and waves them as the truck pulls away and disappears over the horizon.

CHAPTER 10

Disappearing Act

When they look for me I'm not here,
when they find me it's not me.

—*Manu Chao*

Yoli was thirty-three and I was thirteen, a gap wide enough
to make our realities distinct in essential ways, but not wide
enough to foreclose our mutual enjoyment of certain things.
We enjoyed, for example, spending afternoons playing
Twenty-one with the kids from the neighborhood, not just
because we liked basketball, but because we enjoyed hearing
those very young boys curse with virtuosity. We also enjoyed
sharing music. We traded tapes and CDs, and sometimes
when we were at home together we would take turns playing
albums or picking radio stations. I think we liked it because
it was a shortcut to learning about each other as people,
about our tastes and pleasures—things that are often lost in
the rigid communion between parents and their children.

There was something alluring about hearing tracks she
was into that were recorded and popular before I was born,
especially tracks I wouldn't have imagined her liking. That
kind of surprise suggested there were many things I didn't
know about her, that there were parts of Yoli's world that
existed beyond me, before me.

One day after school we were hanging out at home, something that happened less and less because she'd started working well into the evenings. A friend, who was a few years older than I was, had given me a tape he'd made, and I played it over and over on a small boom box I kept on my bed for listening to a call-in radio show about sex when I was supposed to be going to sleep. It was a mix of stuff like Jaguares, Molotov, and El Tri. I remember bringing out the boom box—the tape already in it from the previous night—and pressing play. The last third of "Que No Te Haga Bobo Jacobo" blared from the speakers. The track was about Jacobo Zabludovsky, Mexico's first anchorman, who held the overwhelming majority of news viewers for Televisa for three decades starting in 1970, two years after the massacre of students in Tlatelolco by the state. Jacobo, as he came to be known by nearly everyone in Mexico, and by much of Latin America, was also commonly known to be a stooge for the Partido Revolucionario Institucional (PRI), the party that had been in power since the end of the twenties and had been responsible for Tlatelolco. The PRI would go on to run the country for seven uninterrupted decades despite the massacre.

Yoli had been chopping something for dinner, but as soon as she heard the name Jacobo she put the knife down and started following the voice on the boom box. I had no idea who Zabludovsky was at the time. I had a cursory awareness of politics because Martín and Yoli left cartoon books like *Marx para Principiantes* and several other Rius comic books, lying around the house. I'd flipped through them and, because I liked the cartoons and funny captions, I'd also read parts here and there, understanding very little but finding them enjoyable. I remember liking the drawings of Marx's oversized head and beard and the way Rius mashed animation styles on the same page. But the track about Zabludovsky was the first time I got a specific glimpse of a particular political situation.

The next track came on.

"Me llaman el desaparecido—"

Yoli turned from the counter and watched me bobbing my head along with the plinky guitar for a moment before going to the boom box and pressing stop.

"Sabes de qué se trata eso?" she asked, pointing with the kitchen knife.

I don't remember exactly what she said. Her explanation was abridged because I was thirteen, but she didn't completely skip the kind of information that produced a visceral reaction in my body. I had by that time already witnessed drive-by shootings and bodies being mangled in various ways: an arm broken with a baseball bat, a young man kicked unconscious while on the ground by a group, and someone shot in the throat. But this was different. I remember her repetition of *el estado*. *El estado* did this. *El estado* did that. My previous encounters with violence had been traumatic to see, hear, be in the midst of, but all of them were perceived as transgressions, acts that violated the order we lived in. Yoli's explanation didn't square with that, though. She was telling me that those who were in charge of establishing order had committed acts of extreme violence, final acts, against civilian youth, against *estudiantes*, she repeated. I remember feeling the pulse in my fingertips as I sat perfectly still listening to her tell me about bodies being flown out over the ocean and dumped, and about a square lined with sharpshooters opening fire into crowds of students. Folded into her explanation were suggestions that these acts of violence didn't begin and end with what happened to bodies but included what stories were told or not told, and what stories were inscribed in official records.

. . .

Shortly after learning about Tlatelolco, about the enduring Latin American tradition of student massacres, my mom and dad took me to the National Museum of Mexican Art on Nineteenth Street, where we went every few months when I was growing up. It was their way of not only immersing me in representations of our culture and ourselves, but of exposing me to histories and contexts that were often missing in the lessons I learned in school. Each visit they would let me pick something from the gift shop. That time, or some time close to it, I chose a small rectangular refrigerator magnet we kept on our fridge for over a decade. I didn't think much about it at the time. The image on it was of Remedios Varo's painting *Fenómeno*, which she completed in 1962, one year before her death and six years before Tlatelolco. The painting is of a man and his shadow, except the shadow walks upright filling the three-dimensional space of the man while he is confined to the flat parameters of the shadow world.

Much has been written about Varo and her work, most of it centering on the role Freudian symbolism, alchemy, and mysticism played in her painting. She developed a complex network of symbols, a kind of post–World War II allegorical style where the Christian iconography of the High Renaissance was not discarded but destabilized and redeployed. Interpretations of her works abound, and many rest on the primacy of her personal anxieties or resistance to the rigid subordination of women in Parisian Surrealist circles. Many interpretations begin and end there, in the personal psychology of a female agent moving through European intellectual circles commenting insularly, without considering the influence of broader realities on her being. She experienced the beginning of the Spanish Civil War in her late twenties and the outbreak of World War II less than a decade after that, and she landed in Mexico in 1941 during a burgeoning student movement on the steady march toward the Cold War.

Whatever the intended meaning, the production of *Fenó-*

meno in the early sixties in Mexico is remarkable. It serves as a kind of spirit photograph, a depiction of the zeitgeist. It communicates a central phenomenon that would occur throughout Latin America in the following decades: the murder and disappearance of large swaths of the population by the state.

After the desert I go to Agua Prieta, Sonora, to work at a migrant resource center run by a faith-based organization called Frontera de Cristo, staffed mostly by locals and a few volunteers from abroad. Agua Prieta, a town just on the other side of the border of Douglas, Arizona, reminds me of Gary, Indiana, which I'd driven through a few times, always on the way to someplace else. On my first day, a minister with the organization, a white man with wispy blond hair and a calm face, took me to see the plaza, a large empty square in the middle of town, with a few benches and trees but not a soul anywhere. He explained things would probably be slow at the center because people captured in the Tucson sector were being transported hundreds of miles along the border and dumped elsewhere, a practice called lateral repatriation. Often people were repatriated in areas with active cartel warring, like Nuevo Laredo, where the Zetas massacred seventy-two migrants in August 2010. I stay in the Frontera de Cristo trailer in Douglas with another volunteer, and I'm provided a girl's bicycle, small and purple, to ride from the trailer park down the Pan-American Highway and across the border to the resource center.

One morning we ride into downtown Douglas a few hours before our shift to hang out in the public library. Half of Douglas looks like an old-timey tourist trap, and the main strip approaching the border is a concentration of fast-food restaurants and big-box stores. In the library, I pull several books about Latin American art off the shelves and flip through them while drinking my morning coffee. A few minutes later, I come across the familiar image of a long upright shadow—three-dimensional and walking—trailed by a flattened man cast on a few brick steps, as though *he* were the shadow: *Fenómeno*. Seeing it gives me a chill because of the association to forced disappearances it has come to have for me, and because it appears here, like this, now.

For the next few days I can't stop thinking about the painting as I sit in the mostly empty resource center and walk down desolate streets where people struggle to make their lives despite the conditions imposed by the wall and the logic of the states that erected the barrier. One afternoon when I walk into the center—which is really just a narrow hallway with a desk, refrigerator, and small area for donated clothes at the far end—there's a young man in his early twenties who looks like my uncle Pablo sitting in one of the plastic chairs along the wall. He has a square, athletic build and jet-black hair and eyes. Next to him sits a young woman, around the same age, with a long black braid that has the intensity and shine of obsidian. She's wearing overalls and looks to be in the last trimester of pregnancy.

I sit next to them and introduce myself. Angela, the young woman, tells me they're from Oaxaca and had been caught and released that same morning after signing some papers. The area around the actual port of entry, about fifty feet from the migrant center, is a concentration of activity. Adrian, the young man, stands and walks to the doorway of the center and looks out onto a wall of unknown faces, a few cars idling and circling, men waiting to see what comes across the line. Many towns across the border have illicit economies that revolve around kidnapping and extorting migrants, and that's part of the reason the center is in operation, but things have been quiet in Agua Prieta for some time. I walk over and stand with Adrian, looking out onto the clogged street. He nods over at a pickup truck in the middle of the intersection. Standing on the bed of the truck, with his hands on a turret-mounted machine gun, is a federal cop in black tactical gear, black balaclava, and navy fatigues.

I ask Adrian a question I already know the answer to.

"Porque no hay ni como, mano," he answers, walking back to Angela, slipping his hand underneath her overalls and resting his hand on her rounded belly.

"No hay ni como." There isn't even how. How to make a living. How to feed your infant. How to make a life.

Later Adrian shows me a money order for $250. He explains that when they were booked, the folded bills he kept in his shoe were taken, and when they repatriated they were given this money order. He asks if I could go with them to cash it, and I ask if Angela might want to wait at the center, but before I'm even done asking the question, she's already standing beside us, both of them shaking their heads no, firmly hand in hand.

Cashing the money order becomes a task that ends several hours later with me crossing into the United States and going to a branch of my bank about a mile from the border. As I'm going through the port of entry, I pass a turnstile gate and approach a desk with an old white man behind it. He looks hostile until I present my US passport card and answer his question about where I'm going and why in a voice he didn't expect from this body. He stops me short of finishing.

"All right, all right, all right," he says, waving me through.

My crossing takes less than three minutes, and the ease of it horrifies me. Walking toward the bank, I sweat through all my clothes, but I can't really feel the heat because my mind is cycling through Yoli and Martín, Angela and Adrian, Octavio, the group in the desert, and all the people I would never meet, all laboring to find a place in which they can exist.

When I get back it's evening, and I call to arrange a ride

and bed for the couple at a migrant shelter nearby. The later it gets, the more agitated they seem, and it pains me that there's little else I can do. I heat up some food for them—two bean burritos—and give them each an apple. I sit along the row of white plastic chairs, not knowing what to say. They ask me questions about where I live and what I do, how I'd gotten to the United States and when. A squad car is parked in front of the port of entry. We watch dusk turn to night, staring at the red and blue lights blinking on a wall just beyond the door. Angela lays her head in Adrian's lap, and he gently sweeps a few strands of hair from her face.

My shift is over before their ride comes. Adrian shakes my hand and pulls me in for a hug. Angela hugs me and kisses me on the cheek. As I unlock my small bicycle from a short fence just outside, I look back and see an image that burns itself into my memory: Angela, in her long-sleeved shirt and overalls standing the way very pregnant women do, her legs planted just wider than usual, her back slightly bowed, and Adrian standing next to her with one hand under her elbow, the other resting on the small of her back, both of them crowned in white light from the long bare bulbs just overhead.

As I ride back through the port of entry down the Pan-American Highway, it begins to rain. I think about the severity of a woman as pregnant as Angela walking through the desert, about what has to be true in the consciousness of ordinary Americans in order for this to happen, and about how the couple's journey to this place began by being dislodged and displaced from somewhere they used to know as home. The rain picks up, and the stream of water in the gutter in which I'm riding widens suddenly and nearly sweeps the tires out from under me. My first thought is to hope there isn't anyone walking in a wash right now, because surely they'll be swept away. Dogs bark in the distance as I turn off the highway toward the mobile home park. There are no streetlights so I ride the rest of the way in almost total darkness.

That night I have a dream in which I see the face of a man I'd never met. When I wake up in the trailer the following morning I don't remember anything about the dream, anything about what this man I'd conjured looked like, but for some reason I know it was the man whose sweatshirt I'd seen in the desert.

Somewhere between Arivaca and Sasabe I'd taken a long trek with another volunteer to leave gallons of water in a clearing that straddled the international line. The walk there was especially arduous. At a certain point the only way to keep going in the direction we needed to go was to descend a sheer rock face about fifteen feet into an arroyo that looked like it had just settled after the last heavy rain. The bed of the wash was covered in rocks, many of them loose, which ranged between the size of a dog and the size of a truck. For long stretches the brush was so thick we couldn't see where we were stepping, and I found myself praying we wouldn't find a rattlesnake. An hour into the hike we stopped to take a drink from our canteens, crouching into a bit of shade cast by the wall of the wash. There was a shallow puddle between us, with a loam-green film covering the submerged stones and tan water spiders gliding along the surface and, below, small oblong creatures darted along indiscernible paths, leaving small bubbles zigzagging upward in their wakes. I'd been surprised to see how green the desert was when I arrived, and I was surprised again to see so much life teeming in the small puddle. After a few minutes without speaking, my companion, having similar thoughts to mine, said it was a Eurocentric trope to mischaracterize the desert as a place of death: "The O'odham have always lived here. It's not the desert that's doing all the killing."

We continued around a bend and saw a sheer rock face several hundred feet high in the near distance. In front of it there were a few strands of barbed wire stretched between wooden posts that were almost a story high, with enough space between them to maneuver through if you had a partner to pull them apart. In the center of the shoddy fence was a brown sweatshirt snagged from the hood on a high barb, and from a sleeve on a diagonally lower one so that as we approached it looked like a man making his way through. Neither of us said so, but we both thought there was someone there. We were both arrested at the same moment of recognizing a human figure in the distance, and we both started to react as though it were a person, raising one of our gallons of water and quickening our step. To be visible means that we have been seen, or at least the potential to be seen by another exists, and when we are, our existence is confirmed by another's gaze. Whatever body filled that sweatshirt, and whatever life animated that body, refused to be unseen even in its absence. Although I didn't know anything about the person, any of the particularities that make an individual— their name, the place in which they originated, the circum- stances under which they made their journey, the specific contours of their face, their favorite dish, whether or not they had any children, musical tastes, what they enjoyed doing in their free time, the timbre of their voice, the cadence with which they spoke, their wounds and their scars—I knew enough to know that this was no place for that person.

Many South and Central American migrants today are displaced by reverberations of the same military incursions, violence, and instability that produced the desaparecidos during the Cold War proxy wars of the second half of the twentieth century. Mexico's economy and the fate of large portions of its domestic labor force have long been domi- nated by the United States. Most recently NAFTA and other trade agreements implemented in the early to mid- 1990s have had disastrous effects on some of Mexico's most vulnerable populations. A report published by the Carnegie Endowment found that "agricultural trade liberalization linked to NAFTA is the single most significant factor in the loss of agricultural jobs in Mexico" and that by the end of

2002, Mexican agriculture lost 1.3 million jobs. The same report found that "real wages in Mexico are lower today than when NAFTA took effect." By the late 1990s, nearly half of all employed Mexicans were employed in the informal economy, which is vaguely defined by the Organization for Economic Co-Operation and Development as "units engaged in the production of goods or services with the primary objective of generating employment and incomes to the persons concerned," which means chewing gum vendors, street musicians, shoe shiners, squeegee people, and the men and women who sell foam lizards on lengths of wire to tourists, none of whom are considered unemployed. With major job losses, no unemployment insurance (Mexico offers none), and a fall in real wages, rural households already struggling to survive were pushed completely into abject poverty. The first phase in this disappearance is to be made redundant by the economic policies agreed upon by the oligarchs of increasingly "cooperating" states. As a redundancy, one is made invisible in plain sight—that is, invisible to the civic body in which one continues to exist—someone turned into a walking shadow, with the dimensionality of a person but without the possibility of recognition. What happens to migrants in the Sonoran Desert, and long before they get to the desert, is not an accident—it's the letter and spirit of policy. By eschewing realism, one of the things *Fenómeno* prophesizes is the process of this kind of disappearance—one that begins in place, without the vacating of a body.

When one thinks of a shadow, one typically imagines an absence—a type of nothing—but this is fundamentally wrong. In Varo's painting, the visual space where the viewer assumes a man once was, or should be, is occupied by a shadow. The black three-dimensional figure fills the rounded contours of a body, except it is made of darkness. The darkness walks, while the image of the man is relegated to the flat world of silhouette. A shadow is not the absence of light but a relationship of light with itself and with an observer. This is why we can see shadows within shadows and the textures of objects and surfaces upon which shadows are cast. This is why shadows do not exist in totally dark rooms. Nevertheless, our association of shadows with nothingness remains.

Nothing is supposed to signify no one, no place, and no thing—not anything, not at all, no single thing—yet when we investigate what's referred to by *nothing* we invariably find something. In a shadow, for example, there is always light, and it is blue—not always the same blue, because it changes depending on the distances between objects, light sources, and observers, but some light always radiates into the area alleged to be absent of it. If we think about the physical sciences, a vacuum is often synonymous with and supposed to represent a kind of nothing, but even the most sophisticated laboratory equipment and processes cannot evacuate space of everything. In fact, in the discipline of physics, a vacuum is not understood to be nothing, but rather only a space absent of particles with which photons are known to interact. Where we think there is nothing, we always find something.

A disappearance is said to have occurred when something ceases to be visible. In cases of human disappearance, this definition could not be farther from the truth. When a person disappears, the missing becomes hyper-visible, hyper-present. In Argentina the Mothers of the Plaza de Mayo, a group of women whose children were disappeared by the military junta of the 1970s, continue to visit police stations holding worn photographs and articles of clothing of their disappeared children, demanding to know where, what, how, and why. Some of the adolescent siblings of desaparecidos say when their brothers or sisters were taken they were made orphans because their parents disappeared too, psychologically and emotionally, never able to think about anything but the missing, never out of an excruciating cycle of compulsive thoughts. If their disappeared children lived at home, some of the mothers have kept guard over their rooms making sure that not one object is touched or moved, not one open book closed, not one pen capped. Ashtrays sit full for forty years. The missing do not truly disappear until those who surrounded them, those who felt deeply for them one way or another, are gone too.

One of the most common human practices across cultures through millennia is the enactment of funereal rituals that center on the body of the departed. Not everyone buries their dead, but everyone has the need to mark the passage from life to death by acknowledging the evacuation of personhood in viewing the stillness of the body, attempting to ensure happiness in the afterlife by adorning the body, granting safe passage into another world by cleansing the body, forging closure in speaking good-byes to the body, ensuring entrance to the afterlife by anointing the body, precipitating the voyage to another realm by destroying the body. Without the body, the desperate mind latches onto the most unlikely of hope against all reason. Without the body, or at the very least without the knowledge of death having occurred, it is difficult, if not impossible, for loved ones to find closure. The trauma of ambiguous loss is daily inflicted anew. It remains a gaping wound that will never close, never heal, never cease to excruciate. To this day, mothers roam the Atacama, a vast desert spanning 105,000 square kilometers, combing the arid grounds looking for fragments of their sons' and daughters' bones.

The total number of people who have died attempting to cross the US-Mexico border is unknowable. According to Customs and Border Protection there were 6,330 "Southwest border deaths" between October 1, 1998, and September 30, 2014, but this number is all but certainly low. The figures for any given period vary depending on the source. When asked about the discrepancies by a reporter for the *Arizona Republic*, Frank Amarillas, a Border Patrol spokesman for the Tucson sector, said the Border Patrol counts deaths encountered only by agents or deaths referred to them by local law enforcement officials. "We are not notified in every case," he said. Other cases do not meet the narrow criteria for being counted by CBP. William Robbins, Border Patrol spokesman for the Yuma sector, told the *Arizona Republic* that in order to be counted, skeletal remains had to be recovered near the border or on a trail known to be used by migrants. Cases in which local police, private citizens, other migrants, volunteers of civil society organizations, or medical personnel are the first to come in contact with a migrant's remains may not be included in CBP's numbers. It is not common practice or standard operating procedure for CBP to contact local authorities to inquire about found remains.

When the truth of forced disappearances eventually breaches the armor plating of official narratives and begins to be acknowledged, numbers remain a site of contestation. By assigning a number and claiming it represents "Southwest border deaths," CBP is staking a claim in our collective past, present, and future; in history; in individual memory, perception, and evaluation. Rather than reflecting the reality of death due to US policy, the CBP figure much more accurately represents the number of remains recovered in certain arbitrarily and inconsistently determined zones on the US side of the boundary line and, of these, only those for which CBP agents were the first responders. Nevertheless it orients our understanding of reality because it is the official figure. It comes to represent a fair estimate of death along the border. But if we shift just one metric to include estimates for migrants killed in Mexico, the actual human cost of immigration and border policy begins to look radically different. Some civil society groups estimate that the number of migrants disappeared between 2006 and 2012 in Mexico is as high as seventy thousand. If we don't only measure the human cost in fatalities but consider that individuals fit like necessary vectors in family dyads, triads, and so on, that each of these disappearances reverberates beyond the boundaries of the individual, that each represents a missing brother, sister, son, daughter, father, mother, boyfriend, girlfriend, wife, husband, best friend, confidant, or casual lover, the cost begins to feel catastrophic. And it is. It's not uncommon to visit the countryside in Mexico and find all of the men of a certain age are gone, and no one can tell you where they have gone. Families wait each day anticipating communication of any kind, communication that never comes.

Loved ones of the disappeared need to know. The ambiguity becomes so unbearable that some pray simply for the knowledge, the confirmation, that their loved one is dead, but an integral part of this phenomenon is the production and maintenance of ambiguity. For decades after the fact, authorities declared there were no mass graves in Argentina, and that no one had been flown in military planes, drugged, blessed by military chaplains, and dumped into the Río de la Plata off the coast of Buenos Aires. No one had been incinerated. Pope Francis, then known as Jorge Mario Bergoglio, a leader in the Jesuit order of Argentina during the Dirty War, could do nothing, could say nothing. The military dictatorship of Augusto Pinochet did not scatter the remains of anyone in the Atacama. There are no mass graves in Chile. No one was flown over the Pacific and thrown from helicopters. Jute sacks containing bodies were not dumped in lakes and rivers throughout Chile. The Central Intelligence Agency of the United States knew nothing of it. It had not trained Pinochet's army. It had not funded them. The Sonoran Desert is not scattered with unrecovered, unidentified souls. The riverbed of the Rio Grande is not embedded with unidentified family members. There are no mass graves in the United States.

. . .

Before leaving the desert, another volunteer and I had been driving to a remote location when our truck stalled on a hill and wouldn't start. We radioed camp, and another crew said they would drive out to get us. Within two minutes the heat inside the truck became so intense both of us had soaked through our clothes, and I was having trouble drawing breath so we had to step out. Within another minute it became apparent we needed to find shade, but it was noon, so the sun was directly overhead, and everywhere we turned there were nothing but short, thin mesquite trees, barrel cacti, and sotol. We couldn't wait inside the car and, because of the position in which it had become stalled, there was no room to crawl under it. We sat down for a moment in the middle of a small clearing, but again the sun became so intense that my shoulders burned, even through my shirt, and I felt several moments of overwhelming panic. The urge to tear off my clothes cut through reason because it felt like I was suffocating in them, and I remembered hearing that many dead migrants were found naked because in their last moments they'd become crazed with desperation under the savagely brutal sun. I ran to the truck and emptied half a gallon of water over my head. My partner followed, dumping the other half over his. We radioed the other crew again, and they said they were about half an hour away. I remember feeling a pinprick of terror, despite having a truck full of water. Then I remembered I had a large green raincoat in my backpack. I gathered brittle, thorny branches and collected them in a tall pile, throwing the raincoat over the top, making a sort of canopy that produced just enough shade for us to crouch beneath.

As we waited, my temples began to throb, and all I could think about was how this heat and this sun helped make things disappear, how the desert as landscape—preexisting and natural—was a refinement of the torture centers that had existed in places like Chile and Argentina. Those black

sites had been housed in preexisting buildings so that after the deeds were carried out, knowledge of them could be
scrubbed away and the buildings reintegrated into daily life.
The desert was that and more, helping not only to carry out
the deeds but also to obfuscate lines of causality and responsibility. It made those who died in it seem responsible for
their own disappearance.

The final place of unrest for these unidentified dead is
a section of Tucson's Evergreen Cemetery. Most of the
grounds are tree-lined and lush despite the arid climate, but
beyond a certain point the grass ends and there is only hard,
bare dirt. This austere periphery rarely sees mourners; it's
where migrant remains are deposited when no identification
can be made. The area looks like an abandoned lot. There are
two rectangular grave markers on the dirt next to each other,
which read "JOHN DOE UNK 1992" and "JOHN DOE
UNK 1995." Someone stabbed a small bouquet of red plastic flowers between the slabs long ago. The petals have since
been beaten down by annual monsoons and have faded to a
dull pink. In 2004 the county ruled that unidentified remains
found in the desert would be cremated to save space. The
above-ground columbaria look like brown dumpsters, with
ceramic slabs that open to dark niches where the metal boxes
of unclaimed ashes are placed and will remain in ambiguity.

CHAPTER 11

Streamline

An older white stranger in his fifties buys me drinks well into the night. He's one of those lonely types who rambles continuously without stopping, maybe because he lives alone and rarely has occasion to speak aloud. He's saying something about his brother who he hasn't seen in over twenty years because of a fight they had. Around closing time I don't need to let my eyes go crossed for everything to look soft. The bare, hanging bulbs bloom into orbs of light that look like white hydrangeas. When he pays our tab I give him a hug before we part—because he looks like he really wants one. He says he can't remember what the fight was about, but it's too late because they've gone too long hating each other, and now it's just about that hate. "Call your brother," I say before we say good-bye. He gives me a cigarette for the road, and I take off walking down a random street without direction. I feel like walking, and so I do, for hours. I tend to do this in every city I find myself in, wander around at dawn listening to the hollow sounds of urban spaces at night. Tucson has its own pitch, but it also sounds like all the others, like an empty iron hull, similar to putting your ear to a seashell only much grander because this is the rushing static of highways and commerce in the distance. I must have walked for four or five miles before making my way to the house where I'd arranged to stay. I didn't see a soul the whole time.

I open my eyes before my alarm goes off. It's dark and the unfamiliar orientation of the room throws me. Then, just as my eyes adjust to the darkness and I see a white cat staring at me from a window ledge on a redbrick wall, I remember I'm in Tucson.

The woman who hosts volunteers in Tucson lives in an old adobe structure that used to be a market. Five-foot nopales line the front, some of which still have purple fruit on them from the monsoon. The federal courthouse is just a couple blocks away and, as I leave the house, I cut across a parking lot about the size of a football field. In the middle of this huge black lot, I come upon the desiccated remains of a small white scorpion—no larger than a quarter, perhaps crushed underfoot.

In the middle distance, the federal courthouse mars the landscape. It has the look of a research hospital or an urban juvenile prison. I approach a short woman with jet-black hair who stands at the stoplight across the street from the entrance. Her hair is like thick wire, and from behind she looks like my mother, with whom I haven't spoken in weeks. At the desert camp, getting cell phone service required walking up a hill that was heavily patrolled by Border Patrol, so I didn't make any calls. Besides, I would have had to come up with a series of lies about where I was and what I was doing, and she always knows when I'm lying to her.

Inside the federal building a man wearing a blue Civil War uniform walks through the metal detector. It blares harshly, amplified by all the hard surfaces.

"Pewter," he says to the security guard, pointing at his buttons.

Upstairs a handful of individuals silently congregate at the closed door of a courtroom. I recognize an older woman with a shock of gray curls and an elegant gait from a newspaper photo I'd seen of her speaking into a bullhorn in front of this very building. A series of judges' portraits in oil, about a dozen, hang on the wall. Three are men of color. The woman with the gray curls looks powerful. She enters the courtroom first. The rest of us file in behind her.

A tall, brutish man tells us not to communicate in any way with the detainees. A door near the judge's stand opens, and the large hollow chamber is filled with the sound of chains as prisoners shuffle in with their wrists and ankles shackled. Around seventy men and four women are led into the federal courtroom by US marshals. They're chained together in groups of eight and slacks of metal links between them drag across the courtroom floor, crashing over the lip of the threshold to the chamber door. As they file in, the sounds accrete into layers of metal crashing into metal with a constant undertone of dragging and scraping across hard surfaces. It almost becomes rhythmic for moments but quickly slips back into chaos.

It seems as though it can't be real, human beings shackled and led into the federal courtroom on a chain for nothing other than immigration offenses. It feels like I'm watching a historical reenactment, something from the distant past, but Operation Streamline has been touted by some as progress. Even though the particularities of this little-known spectacle are viscerally obscene, it's one of the endpoints we've reached following our bipartisan, foundational assumptions about what a nation-state is and needs to be. There's no humane or ethical way to deny people who live in countries riddled with violence, poverty, and corruption the right to try to make a livable life in "your" affluent country, much less so when "your" country's government has been deeply involved in creating the conditions being fled.

The soundtrack of metal upon metal peaks at an almost intolerable level before some of the men and women sit down in pew-style benches to the left of the judge's stand.

I'm sitting in the fourth row of benches for public observers. My eyes are fixed on the succession of faces emerging into the chamber. One man looks around the courtroom like he's never seen anything like it: the panels on the walls, the towering judge's stand, his fellow prisoners, some of whom are having trouble dragging themselves and their chains to their seats. I've never seen anything like it either. His face is covered in dust and streaked with sweat. He seems slightly confused, as if he doesn't understand where he is or what's happening. A trickle of dry blood has crusted over on his forehead and pooled into a clump at his brow ridge. Another man coughs, and puffs of dust come off his red shirt, lingering in the stagnant courtroom air. He looks like a friend I once worked with, also undocumented, who used to pop his head into the alley when I'd go on smoke breaks and take one drag of my cigarette, then pop back inside because his fiancée, a US citizen who would have slapped him if she'd caught him smoking, worked there too. He'd once drunkenly confessed that when he started dating her, the possibility of getting his citizenship had been in the back of his mind, and he wondered aloud whether he wouldn't have broken up with her a few times when they'd gone through some rough patches in their relationship had her citizenship not been a factor. I told him it sounded like a pretty standard love story to me, and that seemed to appease whatever it was he was feeling.

Most of the detainees' clothing and skin is torn up from brushing against hard, thorny plants in the desert or falling down slopes of jagged and shifting rocks. The air is thick and sour with the sweat of almost a hundred people, some of whom have been traveling for days, sometimes weeks. The stretch of the Sonoran where most of these people were picked up is some of the harshest terrain in North America. Plants and animals in this desert corridor are hearty and designed to protect their water and limited resources, which means features that draw blood and cause pain.

Two court translators look at each other, smirking. One of them whispers something into the other's ear, and they both chuckle. I wonder if they're here every day. They seem to not see the prisoners.

None of the people who are shackled look out toward the observers. I don't know many individuals who like to be observed at all, let alone during situations of great distress. They must know we're not here to help them, how could we, and so they must wonder what the hell we're looking at. Groups of around seventy or eighty people are brought into this courtroom five days a week. A woman I spoke with, who had been to Streamline previously, said she had seen a man who could barely drag himself to his bench. He'd had to be told to be quiet several times during the proceedings because his pained groans echoed in the chamber while the judge read his sentences. It turned out the man had been apprehended after journeying through the desert for something like six days. He'd told the Border Patrol agent who picked him up that he'd fallen and that his leg was radiating agonizing pain like he'd never felt, that he needed to see a doctor, please. He had been told to shut up. He was booked, and he waited several hours before being transported to a holding cell in Tucson, where he asked to see a doctor again, and was again denied. He met with his public defender an hour before going into Streamline, but instead of receiving medical attention he was made to drag himself in to stand trial. He was sentenced along with the rest of his seventy- or eighty-person cohort and transported to the private prison where he would be held. There he was finally seen by a doctor who determined that he had sustained a broken femur, which is considered a life-threatening injury.

· · ·

The men and women look battered. Many have been traveling on foot over severely uneven terrain for days, some have been journeying for weeks, and for some this is not the first border they've crossed. A thick man wearing a navy blue windbreaker that reads "MARSHAL" across the back looks bored as he tells the first batch of eight men to move, pointing to the spot on the floor where he wants the first man. My temples are pounding, and I can feel my heart beating in my neck. The sound of their chains fills the courtroom again as they shuffle out of the pew. It seems so obviously wrong to shackle and batch-litigate groups like this that I can't believe it's been deemed legitimate, that rather than this scene being a violation of any law it *is* the law in practice.

The marshal doesn't look into the detainees' eyes as they file by close enough to lean forward and kiss him. His face is relaxed and emotionless as he leads them forward to stand before the judge. The translators put on their headsets, and when the detainees are standing in a line facing the judge their public defenders line up behind them. For most, today is the first and last time these public defenders will see their clients, and because of the sheer number of people processed every day, they get about twenty minutes with each.

The third prisoner looks younger than me, maybe even a minor. He has trouble walking in a straight line. His wide-leg jeans are covered in dust and are so wide they look almost like a dress. I remember having a pair just like them in the early nineties, with a stitched red stripe down the side of each leg. I find myself wanting him to turn and see me seeing him, but I have no idea what I'd do if he actually did, or if my presence here would mean anything to him. The chained men line up behind a long desk facing the judge. Their attorneys stand behind them, and some help the men with getting their headsets on for translation. They'll hear everything the judge is saying in Spanish, but with only minutes between them and their attorneys, there's only the slimmest chance any of them understand what's really happening. The lawyers have little time to do anything except tell them to take the plea and outline what will happen. They don't interview them to document any trauma they may have suffered or any violent crimes they may have witnessed or been subject to, both of which would give them a shot for a non-immigrant U Visa. In exchange for their guilty plea, first-time offenders will not serve any jail time and will not be charged with any felonies or crimes associated with human trafficking or document fraud.

The bailiff tells everyone to stand or remain standing. The judge, a middle-aged white woman, walks into the courtroom holding some papers and takes her seat. The prisoners are told to raise their right hand and are sworn in. The first eight are processed in a matter of minutes. They mostly listen as the judge reads from her papers and doles out predetermined sentences. Three of the men in the first group are being charged with unauthorized reentry. They'll avoid felonies as part of the plea agreement, but they'll be given anywhere from thirty days to six months additional jail time. Most likely they'll serve it in a private Corrections Corporation of America (CCA) prison. Before sending them off, the judge chastises the men in a way that seems practiced and unfeeling. Why hadn't they done it the right way? This is a country of laws she tells them. She says she expects they've learned their lesson.

"Good luck to you all. I hope you have no more trouble," she says.

Just before they're taken away, she reminds the men who've already served their time and have had no time added that this doesn't mean they'll go free. "You'll be released to Immigration authorities and I'm not sure how long it will take to arrange transport to your country of origin, but you will no longer be held on *this* charge," she tells them.

Immigration authorities will hand the men over to CCA,

where they'll be held for however long their sentence is and then continue to be held indefinitely and no longer under any charge. Over the past two decades the number of sentences doled out in federal courts has boomed dramatically, from 36,564 in 1992 to 75,867 in 2012, and this growth has mainly been the result of one particular offense: unlawful reentry to the United States. That means that this felony offense alone accounts for a 48 percent increase in the total number of sentences handed out by federal courts. A US marshal standing by one of the courtroom walls opens the same chamber door the detainees emerged from earlier, and another one leads the chained men to it. I look at each one of their faces as they disappear beyond the threshold. I can't imagine anyone in the courtroom actually thinks their troubles are anywhere close to over. The chamber door slams shut behind them.

I scan the rows, looking for the faces of the men from Puebla we'd encountered just two days ago on the side of the road. I don't think I see them, but when I try to recall their faces, all I can manage is a fuzzy approximation. I remember we sat by a mesquite tree, and I remember we'd shared a genuine moment, where we recognized each other's full and complicated humanity, and that the truth of what happened won't ever be forgotten. The harder I try to bring their faces into focus, the more they seem to shift to looking like members of my family. I remember their faces had seemed warm and youthful to me and that they were tense until I told them my mother was from Puebla. They aren't among the prisoners, I'm certain, because if they were I know we would recognize each other. They may have been here yesterday, maybe even the day before, or perhaps they'll be here tomorrow.

A human life is a totality, so much so that no matter how much we know about a person or a loved one, the individual retains a sublime kernel of mystery that seems to bloom whenever we really look at it. Eighty of them are processed here, like this, every day. Several rounds of people are processed within minutes. It reminds me of a meat grinder, and the justice seems construed solely as predetermined punishment. A detainee raises his hands, one clasped inside the other as if saying a prayer, but he's only going to scratch his nose. His small movements ring throughout the courtroom because of his chains. Another man, who looks to be in his late thirties, who was caught reentering for the fifth time, answers the judge in fluent, nearly unaccented English. Stained nearly completely brown, his billowy white T-shirt hangs on his body, heavy with several days of dried sweat and sand. His arms have the sinewy, dried-out look of someone who labors many hours of most days. Likely he lived somewhere in the United States for years, maybe decades, before being picked up for a moving violation, DUI, or maybe one night he punched someone for a good reason, very little reason, or no reason at all. Judging from how old he looks, he may have had a family wherever he lived, and this might be his continued attempt to rejoin them because he won't give up on being with them. From her elevated bench, the judge, shrouded in black, looks like those old etchings of plague doctors. She sentences the sinewy man to 180 days in prison, after which he'll remain in detainment as the state arranges for his removal.

The US marshal approaches one of the migrant women and motions for her to stand. Her first attempt is unsuccessful: she gets her body off the bench only a couple of inches before she falls back. The majority of Latin American migrants to the United States are working-age men, but women's journeys are often more brutal because of the structural vulnerabilities built into their lived experience. It's possible that one or several of the women who will be made to stand before the judge today have suffered some form of sexual violence on their journey here. There is a dearth of reliable statistics regarding this aspect of migrant women's experience because of institutional disregard, the difficulty of compiling this kind of data due to the clandestine nature of the journey, and because of underreporting for various reasons. Women who do come in contact with authorities are treated as criminals, and their well-being is of no concern to state actors, so they're often quickly processed and deported without any appraisal of what they might have suffered on their way here, as is likely the case with these women here today. Those who are successful in their crossing attempts tend not to report sexual violence because of well-founded fear that going to authorities will end in their deportation. Regarding Central and South American women and girls in transit to the United States, a report published by Amnesty International found, "It is a widely held view—shared by local and international NGOs and health professionals working with migrant women—that as many as six in ten migrant women and girls are raped."

It should go without saying that the suffering of migrant women doesn't end at the border. A recent investigation by PBS found countless women who work as field hands in the United States suffer sexual assault and rape by supervisors, hiring managers, foremen, and other field hands. Many of the women who were interviewed by PBS reported their experience of sexual violence in the fields had been continuous because the perpetrators were either in positions of power or they exploited the women's immigration status and fear of deportation to keep them quiet. Undocumented women who are stalked or physically abused by spouses and partners find themselves trapped, without recourse, because even though these women technically have the right to seek help from the police and social services, these possible interventions are often trumped by punitive legislation aimed at punishing immigration offenders. What little attention is given to the sexual, physical, emotional, and psychological victimization of undocumented women often focuses on the individual actors involved. The aforementioned Amnesty International report found the perpetrators of sexual assaults weren't only coyotes, as official narratives would suggest, but also other migrants, state officials, and law enforcement agents. The few media narratives that focus on the individual perpetrators of sexual violence against migrant women before, during, and after their border crossings invariably have certain racial and ethnic trends arise in their stories without interrogating why. The first sentence of an article published by *Fusion* under the heading "JUSTICE" reads: "Before they can reach the American Dream, many migrant women have to survive a Mexican nightmare." But it would be incorrect to assume this nightmare begins or ends in Mexico or that these racial trends have any bearing on a perpetrator's status as a sex offender. If we draw on the mountains of evidence that exist regarding sexual violence, we would understand that if any ethnic or racial group of women is isolated for consideration, these trends invariably arise, because sexual assault, like most other forms of violent crime, is intra-racial. Studies have also consistently shown that violence against women, committed by men, cuts across racial, ethnic, and socioeconomic status: that poor men, like rich men, rape women; that Mexican men, just like white men in the United States, rape women. This means that if undocumented women suffer more sexual violence than women in general, it is most likely due to other factors, like the power imbalances built into clandestine situations of migration, and the added structural vulnerabilities created by the gendered experience of undocumentedness, both of which arise as a matter of policy.

"Is everyone here pleading guilty because they're guilty?" asks the judge.

One public defender adjusts the black headset on one of the prisoners so he can clearly hear the voice of the translator. If he doesn't speak good enough English to understand, this is maybe the most helpful thing the public defender will do for him.

"Sí," say the men and woman.

"Yes," says one of the men.

His public defender leans over and instructs him to answer in Spanish.

"Sí," he says.

"All answer 'yes,'" says the interpreter.

I wonder how things that are so self-evidently farcical—so absent of any legitimate orientation toward justice—can be called justice. These chambers, the robes, the pomp, the ceremony—for what? I wonder what the judge believes she's doing, if she doesn't realize she's nothing but a manager for labor flows, part of the mechanism that wrings work and political capital from these human beings and their families in the form of suffering and exploitation.

Attorneys have instructed each detainee to take a plea deal, a deal that has been influenced by many individuals, except for the detainees. The judge will ask each group of eight if they understand what's happening, and they'll all answer in the affirmative, even if some of them don't. It's clear to me that at least one man before the judge speaks an indigenous language and only speaks enough Spanish to parrot the other prisoners. Out of nearly eighty people, only one man refuses to enter a plea of guilty. He refuses angrily. The judge dispassionately informs him that he'll be held in detention without bail for an indeterminate amount of time. A thick-necked US marshal unchains him from the other prisoners and leads him out of the courtroom. In their plea agreements, the prisoners have been made to forego their right to a trial, not that a trial would help them, and to engage in a kind of theater of adjudication where everything has already been decided for all of them. No one has been thoroughly interviewed by his or her attorney, and no one will be. The women will not meet with trained crisis counselors who might be able to build a case for a U visa. This is an assembly line, a charnel house for justice's hollow bones.

Each person in the court will have "illegal entry" put on his or her permanent record, a record that through technology is becoming ubiquitous and impossible to ever outmaneuver. They have all had their biometric data captured by having their fingertips digitally scanned and linked to each blemished record so that their own bodies can and will be used against them by the state. Programs like Secure Communities (now defunct) cross-reference booking data at local precincts and federal databases so that any immigration discrepancy would mean being detained for up to two extra business days without charge while ICE agents were sent to get you. The program was recently discontinued because it failed in its stated goal of improving public safety. The Obama administration touted the program's discontinuation as part of so-called immigration reform, but the program was drastically expanded during Obama's first two years in office. In 2008, when George W. Bush was still in office, Secure Communities was operational in fourteen jurisdictions throughout the country. By 2013, all 3,181 jurisdictions (within fifty states, the District of Columbia, and five US territories) were cooperating with the Department of Homeland Security's deportation regime. Eliminating specific programs without changing the underlying conditions in which they exist leaves the door open for this back and forth, which generates political capital according to what's needed at the time by the party in charge.

The same US marshal stands motionless, staring into the middle distance until it's his time to retrieve another group of chained prisoners. He stands too close to a seated detainee and gestures for him to rise by placing his hand horizontally in front of the man's line of sight and moving it upward. He points his index finger at the spot on the ground where he wants him to stand, and then he traces the path he wants him to follow with the same finger. One prisoner looks underage, one is clearly in physical pain, another struggles to keep his eyes open. When they get to their places behind the table, their public defenders put the headsets on their clients' ears and stand behind them doing nothing. The judge reads through the same script. The prisoners answer in the affirmative. The translators translate. The public defenders continue doing nothing. More scripts. A built-in space for the judge to say a few "in-the-moment" words. As with each group, she reprimands this one, some might say gently, for "not doing it the right way." I guess she means that if only they had decades to wait, or a million US dollars to buy an EB-5 (a visa for immigrant investors), they wouldn't be taken away in shackles.

As the court is drained of people, it becomes so quiet that every small sound seems heightened, acute. The dragging and crashing of the chains is so crisp I can almost feel the materiality that produces each sound, the footfall of each measured step the US marshal takes. The short squeak his rubber boot heels produce as he pivots. The stressed breath working its way through each of the prisoners' tensed bodies. High-pitched aspirations through swollen, irritated, dried-out passages. Aspirations through teeth. The concussion of the chamber door slamming shut.

Streamline is a grotesque spectacle. One of the cat's nine tails. An added layer through which migrants are churned to further criminalize their movements and compound their bodily and psychological sufferings. Even if Streamline weren't here, something else slightly more "palatable" would be. Even if judges had the power to use their discretion, their discretion would often conclude similarly. The stenographer stops hitting her keys. The translators remove their headsets. A US marshal motions for the few observers to exit the court. Tomorrow it will all happen exactly as it did today.

There's a small group of dedicated people who gather here

from time to time to block buses from leaving the facility, but the majority, the "white moderate," is always elsewhere, watering his or her lawn, going to indie shows, attending gallery openings to appreciate Mexican-themed art. They never make it down here.

The sun is so glaring, the sky looks like a glittering opal. It's lovely. My mouth becomes a faucet and black creeps in from the edges of my field of vision. When I can see again, I'm holding onto the top of a metal trashcan, looking down into a pool of my saliva soaking into a cardboard pizza box. I look up to the street where a young white girl, maybe five, wearing an oversized green bow in her hair, walks down the sidewalk holding her father's hand, while inside the people who've just been processed are loaded onto buses and will be locked in cages for attempting to get what she was given at birth.

ACKNOWLEDGMENTS

My partner, Caitlin Roach, spent many mornings, afternoons, and evenings grinding away at drafts of this manuscript with me. Without her curiosity, economy of language, ferocious intelligence, and love, this book would not exist. Conversations and interactions with countless individuals helped me to better see the truth of my situation and the situations of others like me. I would like to acknowledge the essential work being done by groups like No More Deaths, Frontera de Cristo, and the Colibrí Center for Human Rights. Individuals involved in those groups showed me what it means to live in solidarity with others. Thank you.

Thank you to Octavio for transgressing and living, despite so many things. Thank you to Yoli and Martín for always fighting for me and for each other. Thank you to Yoli, in particular, who taught me that all information needs to be interrogated, especially information presented as truth, and most especially truth presented by authority. Thank you to David Lazar for encouraging me to trust my mind and spirit on the page. Thank you to Jeff Porter, John D'Agata, Robin Hemley, and Patricia Foster for helping me hone my voice, and for the support they've given me throughout this project. Thank you to my agent, Rob McQuilkin, and editor,

Gayatri Patnaik, who believed in this project from the beginning. Thank you to all the people who live and breathe resistance. The courage, integrity, and rage of the people I've lived among, loved, and struggled with, made this book.

NOTES

General Note

Many names and identities have been obscured in a variety of ways and to varying degrees. Some locations were visited multiple times. The narrative of this memoir suggests that things progressed in a linear fashion, which was generally the case, but some spans of time were compressed for narrative purposes.

Chapter 1: Imaginary Lines

Page 2: The Sig Sauer website states, "The P229® DAK™ is the standard pistol of the Dept. of Homeland Security and the U.S. Coast Guard who selected the P229 after a 3 million round grueling torture test. A favorite among law enforcement professionals, the P229 offers compact size, choice in firepower of 9mm, .357 SIG or .40 S&W, tactical versatility of an accessory rail, double-action only and the unbeatable performance that only comes from SIG SAUER® all in one package." The Secret Service is couched within the Department of Homeland Security, as are the US Immigration and Customs Enforcement (ICE), Customs and Border Protection (CBP), and the US Citizenship and Immigration Services (USCIS). These three latter agencies make up the immigration apparatus of the federal government. Generally ICE is the investigative branch that handles investigations, apprehensions, and raids in the interior of the country. CBP handles the so-called border, even though the border has been made to extend well into the landmass of the country (as will be discussed later). USCIS acts as the administrative branch.

Page 2: The forty-five-cubic-inch temporary stretch cavity is based on Evan Marshall and Edwin Sanow, *Stopping Power: A Practical Analysis of the Latest Handgun Ammunition* (Boulder, CO: Paladin, 2001), 75.

Page 2: An educated guess about what kind of mobile device the Secret Service likely uses to send electronic messages was based on information found in Suzanne Choney, "Obama Gets to Keep His BlackBerry," NBC News, January 22, 2009, http://www.nbc news.com/id/28780205/ns/technology_and_science-tech_and _gadgets/t/obama-gets-keep-his-blackberry/#.VfcxU2RViko.

Page 2: Obama family Secret Service code names: "11 Great Secret Service Code Names," *Time*, n.d., http://content.time.com/time /specials/packages/article/0,28804,1860482_1860481_1860422,00 .html.

Page 5: It should be clear that I have no idea if the "two men at table fifty-six" were actually Secret Service agents.

Page 6: The "three ten bar," as it is colloquially referred to, is still in effect. It is now possible for some qualifying individuals to apply for a waiver. Under the current law, spouses and children of US citizens and lawful permanent residents are allowed to apply for a waiver of the bar before leaving the country for consular interviews if they can demonstrate that their departure would result in "extreme hardship to a U.S. citizen or lawful permanent spouse or parent." The most current information about the bar can be found on the application itself, which at the time of publication of this book could be found here, "Instructions for Application for Waiver of Grounds of Inadmissibility," I-601, US Citizenship and Immigration Services, http://www.uscis.gov/i-601. At the time of my writing this chapter, Octavio would not have qualified for this waiver.

Pages 8 and 9: "Border Insecurity; Criminal Illegal Aliens; Deadly Imports; Illegal Alien Amnesty," Transcripts, CNN, April 14, 2005, http://www.cnn.com/TRANSCRIPTS/0504/14/ldt.01.html.

Page 10: I drew statistics regarding leprosy cases in the United States from what I believed to be the most reliable source, "Hansen's Disease Data & Statistics," graph D, US Department of Health and Human Services, Health Resources and Services Administration, http://www.hrsa.gov/hansensdisease/dataandstatistics.html.

Chapter 2: Martín y Yoli

Page 15: The Reagan quote is from his "Statement on Signing the Immigration Reform and Control Act of 1986," November 6, 1986, Ronald Reagan Presidential Library and Museum, http://www .reagan.utexas.edu/archives/speeches/1986/110686b.htm.

Page 20: My summation and interpretation of the history of US-Mexican relations during the early part of the twentieth century was based on information found in Francisco Balderrama and Raymond Rodriguez, *Decade of Betrayal: Mexican Repatriation in the 1930s* (Albuquerque: University of New Mexico Press, 2006), 60–101.

Page 20: Information and quotes about the Mexican Repatriation comes from California's Apology Act for the 1930s Mexican Repatriation Program (SB 670), enacted in 2005, ftp://www.leginfo .ca.gov/pub/05-06/bill/sen/sb_0651-0700/sb_670_bill_20051007 _chaptered.html.

Page 20: William Kenaston Jr., oral history from Carlos Larralde and Richard Griswold del Castillo, "San Diego's Ku Klux Klan 1920–1980," *Journal of San Diego History* 46, nos. 2 and 3 (Spring/Summer 2000), http://www.sandiegohistory.org/journal /2000-2/klan.htm.

Page 21: William Carrigan and Clive Webb, "The Lynching of Persons of Mexican Origin or Descent in the United States, 1848 to 1928," *Journal of Social History* 37, no. 2 (Winter 2003): 411–38.

Pages 22 and 23: US-Mexican relations, including two quotes ("By the dawn of the twentieth century"): Gilbert González, and Raúl Fernandez, "Empire and the Origins of Twentieth-Century Migration from Mexico to the United States," *Pacific Historical*

Review 71, no. 1 (February 2002): 19–57. My summation and interpretation is also informed by Janice Lee Jayes, *The Illusion of Ignorance: Constructing the American Encounter with Mexico, 1877–1920* (Lanham, MD: University Press of America, 2011); "identical aims and ideals" is from page 128 and the horrendous conditions under the Porfiriato are from page 129.

Page 23: Percentages of oil output by Mexican Eagle Company and Jersey Standard and Standard Oil Company of California: "Milestones: 1937–1945: Mexican Expropriation of Foreign Oil, 1938," US Department of State, Office of the Historian, https://history.state.gov/milestones/1937-1945/mexican-oil.

Page 35: ACLU recommendation: *Know Your Rights: When Encountering Law Enforcement*, American Civil Liberties Union, https://www.aclu.org/files/kyr/kyr_english.pdf.

Page 35: New York Times figures regarding deportations based on minor infractions: Ginger Thompson and Sarah Cohen, "More Deportations Follow Minor Crimes, Records Show," *New York Times*, April 6, 2014, http://www.nytimes.com/2014/04/07/us/more-deportations-follow-minor-crimes-data-shows.html.

Page 36: The "1.7 million" figure comes from Monica L. Heppel and Sandra L. Amendola, *Immigration Reform and Perishable Crop Agriculture: Compliance or Circumvention?* (Lanham, MD: University Press of America, 1992), 23.

Page 36: The $185 fee and criteria for qualifying come from my own family's paperwork.

Page 36: Information about the declawed employer sanctions imposed under the IRCA is based on Nicholas Laham, *Ronald Reagan and the Politics of Immigration Reform* (Westport, CT: Praeger, 2000), 22–75.

Page 39: The number of people who applied for relief under the agricultural worker criteria, 1.3 million, comes from Rachel L. Swarns, "Failed Amnesty Legislation of 1986 Haunts the Current Immigration Bills in Congress," *New York Times*, May 23, 2006, http://www.nytimes.com/2006/05/23/washington/23amnesty.html.

Page 40: The quoted paperwork verification requirement comes from "Immigration Reform and Control Act of 1986," Equal Employment Opportunity Commission, http://www.eeoc.gov/eeoc /history/35th/thelaw/irca.html. Information about what it would take the Justice Department to prosecute employers: Laham, *Ronald Reagan and the Politics of Immigration Reform*, 151. Ronald Reagan quotation: "Statement on Signing the Immigration Reform and Control Act of 1986," November 6, 1986, Ronald Reagan Presidential Library and Museum, http://www.reagan.utexas.edu /archives/speeches/1986/110686b.htm.

Pages 41 and 42: My interpretation and summation of US involvement in Guatemala is based on Stephen M. Streeter, "Guatemala," in *Encyclopedia of U.S. Military Interventions in Latin America*, ed. Alan L. McPherson (Santa Barbara: ABC-CLIO, 2013), 251–54; quotes regarding communication of knowledge of massacres in Guatemala: Daniel Wilkinson, *Silence on the Mountain: Stories of Terror, Betrayal, and Forgetting in Guatemala*, American Encounters/Global Interactions (Durham: Duke University Press, 2004), 326–27.

Page 42: Truth commission report: *Guatemala: Memory of Silence*, Commission for Historical Clarification, 1999.

Chapter 3: Biometrics

Page 45: This chapter was written before Edward Snowden's disclosures, before mass surveillance had become a verifiable reality in the public consciousness. The type of surveillance and administration immigrants are subject to are more direct and more immediately consequential than the general population experiences. That is not to suggest that any amount of unwarranted surveillance is acceptable.

Page 55: My characterization of the post-9/11 "top-secret architecture" comes from Dana Priest and William M. Arkin, "A Hidden World, Growing beyond Control," Washington Post, July 19, 2010.

Page 55: US-VISIT and Accenture: "US-VISIT Documents, FOIA Electronic Reading Room," Department of Homeland Security,

http://www.dhs.gov/us-visit-documents-foia-electronic-reading
-room. Quotes regarding US-VISIT's current capabilities and goals
for the future: *Biometric Standards Requirements for US-VISIT*,
Department of Homeland Security, 2010, http://www.dhs.gov
/xlibrary/assets/usvisit/usvisit_biometric_standards.pdf.

Page 59: LAPD Suspicious Activity Report program: "More About
Suspicious Activity Reporting," American Civil Liberties Union,
https://www.aclu.org/more-about-suspicious-activity-reporting;
"Information Sharing Environment (ISE); Functional Standard
(FS); Suspicious Activity Reporting (SAR)"; Information Sharing Environment, https://www.ise.gov/sites/default/files/ISE-FS
-200_ISE-SAR_Functional_Standard_V1_5_Issued_2009.pdf.

Page 61: Quote about Tasty Tacos: "Our Story," Tasty Tacos, http://
www.tastytacos.com/history.html.

Chapter 4: La Soledad de Octavio
Pages 63 and 70: Quotes from Paz: Octavio Paz, *The Labyrinth of
Solitude* (New York: Grove, 1985), 195–212.

Page 71: Massumi quotes: Brian Massumi and Gregory J. Seigworth,
"The Future Birth of the Affective Fact," in *The Affect Theory Reader*,
ed. Melissa Gregg (Durham: Duke University Press, 2010), 52–70.

Page 73: Panopticon: Michel Foucault, *Discipline and Punish: The
Birth of the Prison* (New York: Pantheon, 1977), 207.

Chapter 5: A Civilized Man
Page 82: Andrea Mantegna: Andrew Martindale, "The Middle Age
of Andrea Mantegna," Selwyn Brinton Lecture, *Journal of the Royal
Society of Arts*, 627–42; Medici: "The Father of Leveraged Finance:
Cosimo di Giovanni de Medici," Global Sage, http://www.global
sage.com/pdf/track_record_10.pdf.

Page 85: Same-sex immigration relief: Julia Preston, "For Gay Immigrants, Marriage Ruling Brings Relief and a Path to a Green
Card," *New York Times*, July 17, 2015.

Chapter 6: Good Moral Character

Page 88: Deportable offenses after 1996: "Analysis of Immigration Detention Policies," American Civil Liberties Union, https://www .aclu.org/analysis-immigration-detention-policies.

Page 91: Sex industry in the Philippine gross national product: Janice G. Raymond, *Not a Choice, Not a Job: Exposing the Myths about Prostitution and the Global Sex Trade* (Washington, DC: Potomac, 2013), 133,

Page 93: "Theater of libido": Alphonso Lingis, *Abuses* (Berkeley: University of California Press, 1994), 115.

Page 93: Amerasians in the Philippines: Ted Regencia, "No Way Home for Filipino 'Amerasians'" *Al Jazeera English*, April 25, 2014, http://www.aljazeera.com/indepth/features/2014/04/no-way -home-filipino-amerasians-philippines-military-base-201442 57129226765.html; preferential treatment for certain Amerasians: "Definition of Terms," Department of Homeland Security, http:// www.dhs.gov/definition-terms.

Page 95: The beginning of the Philippine Revolution and the role of the Irreconcilables: John A. Larkin, "The Place of Local History in Philippine Historiography," *Journal of Southeast Asian History* 8, no. 2 (1967): 306; Paolo E. Coletta, "Bryan, McKinley, and the Treaty of Paris," *Pacific Historical Review* 26, no. 2 (1957): 131–46; Renato Constantino, *The Philippines: A Past Revisited* (Quezon City: Tala Services, 1975).

Pages 96, 97, and 99: Indigenous resistance to missionaries: Alfred W. McCoy, "Baylan: Animist Religion and Philippine Peasant Ide-ology," *Philippine Quarterly of Culture and Society* 10, no. 3 (1982): 141–94.

Pages 96 and 97: Magellan and rajah of Cebu: Nick Joaquin, "Lapu-Lapu and Humabon: The Filipino as Twins," *Philippine Quarterly of Culture and Society* 7, nos. 1–2 (1979): 51–58.

Page 99: Philippine peasant revolts: McCoy, "Baylan"; Joaquin, "Lapu-Lapu."

Page 103: Moro Sultanates: Astrid S. Tuminez, "Neither Sovereignty nor Autonomy: Continuing Conflict in the Southern Philippines," *Proceedings of the Annual Meeting* (American Society of International Law) 102 (2008): 122–25.

Page 106: Eduardo Murphy Cojuangco Jr.: Carlos H. Conde, "In Philippines, Political Clans Hold Their Ground," *New York Times,* May 20, 2004.

Page 107: Theodore Roosevelt: John B. Judis, *The Folly of Empire: What George W. Bush Could Learn from Theodore Roosevelt and Woodrow Wilson* (New York: Scribner, 2004), 60.

Chapter 7: Ceremony

Page 113: Postville: Spencer S. Hsu, "Immigration Raid Jars a Small Town," *Washington Post,* May 18, 2008.

Pages 116 and 117: Herbert Hoover birth cottage and Isis statue: "Herbert Hoover National Historic Site, Iowa," National Park Service, http://www.nps.gov/heho/index.htm.

Page 117: The quote "physical proof of the unbounded opportunity of American life," was taken from ibid.

Page 118: Quote and discussion of Isis in relation to Athena: "Isis and Osiris," part 1 of 5, in Plutarch's *Moralia,* Bill Thayer's website, University of Chicago, http://penelope.uchicago.edu/Thayer/E /Roman/Texts/Plutarch/Moralia/Isis_and_Osiris*/A.html.

Page 118: Obama breaking deportation records: Ana Gonzalez-Barrera and Jens Manuel Krogstad, "U.S. Deportations of Immigrants Reach Record High in 2013," October 2, 2014, Pew Research Center, http://www.pewresearch.org/fact-tank/2014/10/02/u-s -deportations-of-immigrants-reach-record-high-in-2013.

Page 119: Hoover and the Mexican Repatriation: Apology Act for the 1930s Mexican Repatriation Program (SB 670).

Page 124: "The Universal Declaration of Human Rights," United Nations, http://www.un.org/en/documents/udhr.

Page 125: "Kill program" deemed legal: Tara McKelvey, "Interview with Harold Koh, Obama's Defender of Drone Strikes," *Daily Beast*, April 8, 2012, http://www.thedailybeast.com/articles/2012/04/08/interview-with-harold-koh-obama-s-defender-of-drone-strikes.html.

Page 126: Customs and Border Patrol figure of 365 migrant deaths in the Southwest in 2010: "U.S. Border Patrol Fiscal Year Southwest Border Sector Deaths (FY 1998–FY 2014)," US Customs and Border Protection, http://www.cbp.gov/document/stats/us-border-patrol-fiscal-year-southwest-border-sector-deaths-fy-1998-fy-2014.

Page 127: South and Central American migrants kidnapped in a six-month period: "More Than 11,000 Migrants Abducted in Mexico," *BBC News*, February 23, 2011, http://www.bbc.com/news/world-latin-america-12549484.

Page 127: "Ninety thousand tons of bombs": Thomas George Weiss, *Political Gain and Civilian Pain: Humanitarian Impacts of Economic Sanctions* (Lanham, MD: Rowman & Littlefield, 1997), 93.

Chapter 8: Friendship Park, USA
Page 130: Crime rates among the foreign-born versus native-born populations: "The Criminalization of Immigration in the United States," American Immigration Council, July 8, 2015, http://immigrationpolicy.org/special-reports/criminalization-immigration-united-states.

Page 133: Solana Beach demographics: "Solana Beach (city), California," State and County QuickFacts, US Census Bureau, http://quickfacts.census.gov/qfd/states/06/0672506.html.

Page 133: Rancho Santa Fe: "Million-dollar Zip Codes," *CNNMoney*, http://money.cnn.com/pf/features/lists/million_zips.

Page 134: Sidney Franklin: Bart Paul, *Double-Edged Sword: The Many Lives of Hemingway's Friend, the American Matador Sidney Franklin* (Lincoln: University of Nebraska Press, 2009).

Page 134: Pat Nixon quote ("I hope there won't be a fence"): Todd Miller, *Border Patrol Nation: Dispatches from the Front Lines of Homeland Security* (San Francisco: City Lights, 2014), 25.

Page 134: "Welded metal landing mats": "Background to the Office of the Inspector General Investigation," Office of the Inspector General, https://oig.justice.gov/special/9807/gkp01.htm.

Page 135: Much of the information regarding the similarities between H.R. 1417 and S. 744 comes from "An Unlikely Couple: The Similar Approaches to Border Enforcement in H.R. 1417 and S. 744, American Immigration Council, July 2013, http://www.immigrationpolicy.org/sites/default/files/docs/hr_1417_v_s_744.pdf.

Page 135: Some of the information about the money spent on border enforcement, including the quote, comes from Garrett M. Graff, "The Green Monster." *Politico*, November/December 2014, http://www.politico.com/magazine/story/2014/10/border-patrol-the-green-monster-112220.html.

Page 141: Americans about as likely to be murdered by friends, relatives, and acquaintances as by strangers: Alexia Cooper and Erica L. Smith, *Homicide Trends in the United States, 1980–2008* (Washington: US Department of Justice, Bureau of Justice Statistics, 2011), http://www.bjs.gov/content/pub/pdf/htus8008.pdf.

Page 145: Anastasio Hernandez-Rojas: Randal C. Archibold, "San Diego Police Investigate the Death of a Mexican Man Resisting Deportation," *New York Times*, June 1, 2010; "Crossing the Line at the Border," PBS, May 17, 2013, http://www.pbs.org/wnet/need-to-know/video/border-patrol-part-3/16916; "Transcript: November 30, 2012," *Need to Know*, PBS, November 30, 2012, http://needtoknow.vc2.wnet.org/wnet/need-to-know/transcripts-full-episode/transcript-november-30-2012/15577.

Chapter 9: Passport to the New West

Page 148: Deadliest week in Arizona history: John Fife, "My Tucson: Once Jailed, Pair Become Heroes," *Tucson Citizen*, May 2, 2007. John Fife's criminal history: "Sanctuary Activists Lose Conspiracy Trial," *Chicago Tribune*, May 2, 1986.

Page 150: Border checkpoint figures and their history: *Border Patrol: Available Data on Interior Checkpoints Suggest Differences in Sector Performance* (Washington: Government Accountability Office, 2005), http://www.gao.gov/assets/250/247179.pdf; "The Constitution in the 100-Mile Border Zone," American Civil Liberties Union, https://www.aclu.org/constitution-100-mile-border-zone.

Page 151: CBP agents able to enter private property within twenty-five miles of the border without a warrant: "Know Your Rights With Border Patrol," American Civil Liberties Union of Arizona, http://www.acluaz.org/sites/default/files/documents/ACLU%20Border%20Rights%20ENGLISH.pdf.

Page 152: Border Patrol number for migrant remains recovered on the US side of the boundary in the southwestern sectors: 6,330 between 1998 and 2014. The number of US soldiers killed in Iraq through August 8, 2015 (6,840): "Faces of the Fallen," *Washington Post*, http://apps.washingtonpost.com/national/fallen.

Page 154: Funneling of migrants into the most dangerous parts of the border region: "Border Patrol Strategic Plan: 1994 and Beyond," US Border Patrol, in companion website for Joseph Nevins, *Operation Gatekeeper and Beyond: The War on "Illegals" and the Remaking of the U.S.-Mexico Boundary* (New York: Routledge, 2010), http://cw.routledge.com/textbooks/9780415996945/gov-docs/1994.pdf.

Page 155: NMD footage in "Crossing the Line, Part 2," PBS, July 20, 2012, http://www.pbs.org/wnet/need-to-know/video/video-crossing-the-line/14291.

Pages 155 and 156: All information about abuse in short-term border patrol custody comes from *A Culture of Cruelty: Abuse and Impunity in Short-Term U.S. Border Patrol Custody* (Tucson: No More Deaths, 2011), http://forms.nomoredeaths.org/wp-content/uploads/2014/10/CultureOfCruelty-full.compressed.pdf.

Page 161: Arizona Border Recon: "'Nativist Extremist' Groups Decline Again," Southern Poverty Law Center, February 25, 2014, https://www.splcenter.org/fighting-hate/intelligence-report

/2014/%E2%80%98nativist-extremist%E2%80%99-groups-decline
-again-0.

Page 162: Information about the murders committed by J.T. Ready can be found in Michael Muskal, "Border Guard Founder J.T. Ready Blamed in Arizona Murder-Suicide," *Los Angeles Times,* May 3, 2012. FBI investigation of Ready before he committed the murders: Tim Gaylord, "FBI Investigating Arizona Neo-Nazi Before Shooting," Reuters, May 5, 2012, http://www.reuters.com/article/2012/05/06/us-usa-arizona-shooting-idUSBRE845000 20120506.

Pages 162 and 163: Jeffrey Harbin: "Valley Man Sentenced to 24 Months for Possessing and Transporting Improvised Explosive Devices," press release, Federal Bureau of Investigation, February 7, 2012, https://www.fbi.gov/phoenix/press-releases/2012/valley-man-sentenced-to-24-months-for-possessing-and-transporting-improvised-explosive-devices.

Pages 162 and 163: Shawna Forde: "Arizona Vigilante Found Guilty of Murdering Latino Man, Daughter," CNN, February 15, 2011, http://www.cnn.com/2011/CRIME/02/14/arizona.double.killing.verdict.

Page 163: Russell Pearce on J.T. Ready: "J.T. Ready," Extremist Files, Southern Poverty Law Center, https://www.splcenter.org/fighting-hate/extremist-files/individual/jt-ready.

Page 168: CBP agents killed in the line of duty: "In Memoriam to Those Who Died in the Line of Duty," US Customs and Border Protection, http://www.cbp.gov/about/in-memoriam/memoriam-those-who-died-line-duty.

Page 168: Border Patrol agent suicide: Paul J. Weber, "Increase in Suicides Among Border Patrol Agents Causes Alarm," *Washington Post,* August 19, 2010.

Chapter 10: Disappearing Act

Pages 188 and 189: NAFTA: Sandra Polaski, "Mexican Employment, Productivity and Income a Decade after NAFTA," brief submitted to the Canadian Standing Senate Committee on Foreign Affairs,

Carnegie Endowment for International Peace, February 25, 2004, http://carnegieendowment.org/2004/02/25/mexican-employment -productivity-and-income-decade-after-nafta. Informal economy: *System of National Accounts 1993* (Brussels/Luxembourg: Commission of the European Communities, International Monetary Fund, Organisation for Economic Opportunity and Development, United Nations, World Bank, 1993), http://unstats.un.org/unsD /nationalaccount/docs/1993sna.pdf.

Page 191: The official figure of 6,330 doesn't represent the number of deaths along the border; more accurately it represents the number of remains CBP agents decided to retrieve and count along the Southwest border between October 1, 1998, and September 30, 2014. "U.S. Border Patrol Fiscal Year Southwest Border Sector Deaths (FY 1998–FY 2014)." Regarding possible explanations for the discrepancy in count and difficulty in establishing the real toll of border policy: Susan Carroll and Daniel González, "Border Death Toll Varies Due to Multiple Counting Methods," *Arizona Republic*, October 16, 2003.

Pages 192 and 193: A civil society group estimate of number of migrants disappeared between 2006 and 2012 in Mexico: Ryan Craggs, "Mexico Drug War: Missing Immigrants from Central America Sought by Caravan of Mothers," *Huffington Post*, October 23, 2012, http://www.huffingtonpost.com/2012/10/23/missing-immigrants -mexico_n_2005481.html.

Pages 194 and 195: Black sites in Chile: Karen Elizabeth Bishop, "The Architectural History of Disappearance: Rebuilding Memory Sites in the Southern Cone," *Journal of the Society of Architectural Historians* 73, no. 4 (2014): 612–14.

Chapter 11: Streamline

Page 204: Rise in federal sentences due to immigration criminalization: Michael T. Light, Mark Hugo Lopez, and Ana Gonzalez-Barrera, "The Rise of Federal Immigration Crimes," Hispanic Trends, Pew Research Center, March 18, 2014, http://www.pewhispanic.org/2014/03/18/the-rise-of-federal-immigration-crimes.

Pages 205 and 206: Rape: "Most Dangerous Journey: What Central

American Migrants Face When They Try to Cross the Border," *Human Rights Now Blog*, February 20, 2014, Amnesty International, http://blog.amnestyusa.org/americas/most-dangerous-journey -what-central-american-migrants-face-when-they-try-to-cross -the-border. Sexual violence against field hands: "Rape in the Fields," *Frontline*, PBS, June 25, 2013, http://www.pbs.org/wgbh /pages/frontline/rape-in-the-fields.

Page 207: Quote from *Fusion*: Erin Siegal McIntyre and Deborah Bonello, "Is Rape the Price to Pay for Migrant Women Chasing the American Dream?," *Fusion*, September 10, 2014, http://fusion .net/story/17321/is-rape-the-price-to-pay-for-migrant-women -chasing-the-american-dream. Heterogeneity of rapists: W.L. Marshall and H.E. Barbaree, "Integrated Theory of Etiology of Sexual Offending," in *Handbook of Sexual Assault: Issues, Theories, and Treatment of the Offender* (New York: Plenum Press, 1990), 257–75.

Page 209: Secure Communities: Kate Linthicum, "Obama Ends Secure Communities Program as Part of Immigration Action," *Los Angeles Times*, November 21, 2014; "Secure Communities," US Immigration and Customs Enforcement, http://www.ice.gov /secure-communities.

JOSÉ ORDUÑA was born in Córdoba, Veracruz, and immigrated to Chicago when he was two. At nine, he and his parents traveled to Ciudad Juárez and filed for permanent residency under section 245(i) of the Immigration and Nationality Act. Having entered the United States with a tourist visa, which had since expired, they were considered "removable aliens." In 2010, Orduña applied for naturalization and, in July of 2011, was sworn in as a citizen. He is a graduate of the Nonfiction Writing Program at the University of Iowa and is active in Latin American solidarity.